HIGHER

MODERN STUDIES
2007-2011

2007 EXAM — page 3
2008 EXAM — page 17
2009 EXAM — page 31
2010 EXAM — page 45
2011 EXAM — page 59
ANSWER SECTION — page 75

Publisher's Note

We are delighted to bring you the 2011 Past Papers and you will see that we have changed the format from previous editions. As part of our environmental awareness strategy, we have attempted to make these new editions as sustainable as possible.
To do this, we have printed on white paper and bound the answer sections into the book. This not only allows us to use significantly less paper but we are also, for the first time, able to source all the materials from sustainable sources.

We hope you like the new editions and by purchasing this product, you are not only supporting an independent Scottish publishing company but you are also, in the International Year of Forests, not contributing to the destruction of the world's forests.

Thank you for your support and please see the following websites for more information to support the above statement –

www.fsc-uk.org

www.loveforests.com

© Scottish Qualifications Authority
All rights reserved. Copying prohibited. No part of this publication may be reproduced, stored in a retrieval system, or transmitted in any form or by any means, electronic, mechanical, photocopying, recording or otherwise.

First exam published in 2007.
Published by Bright Red Publishing Ltd, 6 Stafford Street, Edinburgh EH3 7AU
tel: 0131 220 5804 fax: 0131 220 6710 info@brightredpublishing.co.uk www.brightredpublishing.co.uk

ISBN 978-1-84948-222-6

A CIP Catalogue record for this book is available from the British Library.

Bright Red Publishing is grateful to the copyright holders, as credited on the final page of the Question Section, for permission to use their material. Every effort has been made to trace the copyright holders and to obtain their permission for the use of copyright material. Bright Red Publishing will be happy to receive information allowing us to rectify any error or omission in future editions.

HIGHER
2007

X236/301

NATIONAL
QUALIFICATIONS
2007

TUESDAY, 22 MAY
9.00 AM – 10.30 AM

MODERN STUDIES
HIGHER
Paper 1

Candidates should answer **FOUR** questions:

- **ONE** from Section A

and

- **ONE** from Section B

and

- **ONE** from Section C

and

- **ONE OTHER** from **EITHER** Section A **OR** Section C

Section A: Political Issues in the United Kingdom.
Section B: Social Issues in the United Kingdom.
Section C: International Issues.

Each question is worth 15 marks.

SECTION A—Political Issues in the United Kingdom

Each question is worth 15 marks

STUDY THEME 1A: DEVOLVED DECISION MAKING IN SCOTLAND

Question A1

The distribution of reserved and devolved powers means that the most important decisions for Scotland continue to be made at Westminster.

Discuss.

STUDY THEME 1B: DECISION MAKING IN CENTRAL GOVERNMENT

Question A2

To what extent can Parliament control the powers of the Prime Minister?

STUDY THEME 1C: POLITICAL PARTIES AND THEIR POLICIES (INCLUDING THE SCOTTISH DIMENSION)

Question A3

Assess the importance of party unity in achieving electoral success.

STUDY THEME 1D: ELECTORAL SYSTEMS, VOTING AND POLITICAL ATTITUDES

Question A4

The Additional Member System gives voters more choice and better representation than does First Past The Post.

Discuss.

SECTION B — Social Issues in the United Kingdom

Each question is worth 15 marks

STUDY THEME 2: WEALTH AND HEALTH INEQUALITIES IN THE UNITED KINGDOM

EITHER

Question B5

To what extent are the founding principles of the Welfare State being met?

OR

Question B6

To what extent do social and economic inequalities continue to exist in the UK?

[Turn over

SECTION C — International Issues
Each question is worth 15 marks

STUDY THEME 3A: THE REPUBLIC OF SOUTH AFRICA

Question C7

Its political system has all the features of a democracy but South Africa has become a one party state.

Discuss.

STUDY THEME 3B: THE PEOPLE'S REPUBLIC OF CHINA

Question C8

Critically examine the effects of social and economic reform in China.

STUDY THEME 3C: THE UNITED STATES OF AMERICA

Question C9

To what extent do ethnic minorities influence the outcome of elections in the USA?

STUDY THEME 3D: THE EUROPEAN UNION

Question C10

To what extent is there agreement amongst member states on EU social and economic policies?

STUDY THEME 3E: THE POLITICS OF DEVELOPMENT IN AFRICA

Question C11

With reference to specific African countries (excluding the Republic of South Africa):
Foreign aid alone is no guarantee of development.
Discuss.

STUDY THEME 3F: GLOBAL SECURITY

Question C12

Critically examine the effectiveness of international responses to threats to global security.

[END OF QUESTION PAPER]

X236/302

NATIONAL
QUALIFICATIONS
2007

TUESDAY, 22 MAY
10.50 AM – 12.50 PM

MODERN STUDIES
HIGHER
Paper 2

Summary of Decision Making Exercise

You are a social policy researcher. You have been asked to prepare a report for a committee investigating welfare provision in which you recommend or reject the proposal to introduce an Employment and Support Allowance (ESA).

Before beginning the task, you must answer a number of evaluating questions (Questions 1–3) based on the source material provided. The source material is:

SOURCE A: ESA will be fairer

SOURCE B: ESA will increase hardship

SOURCE C: Statistical Information

SOURCE A: ESA WILL BE FAIRER

Incapacity Benefit is meant to provide an income for people who are unable to work because of medical reasons. It is the single most costly benefit that applies to people of working age. The number of people claiming Incapacity Benefit has grown to 2·7 million. Most, but not all of these claimants, are genuinely disabled or suffering from a health condition that prevents them from working. In Scotland, over 300,000 people receive Incapacity Benefit. In Glasgow, one in five of those of working age claim this benefit. Incapacity Benefit increases after six months and again after a year. It is paid for life and may be accompanied by other benefits. Incapacity Benefit discourages people from seeking work. No wonder long-term sickness and disability is the most common reason given by both men and women for not working. It is not just older workers who qualify for Incapacity Benefit — each month over a thousand teenagers claim it. We are encouraging welfare dependency at the expense of individual responsibility. Incapacity Benefit needs reform.

Our proposed Employment and Support Allowance (ESA) will be fairer to new claimants and give the taxpayer better value for their money. It will pay more than Incapacity Benefit but new applicants will face rigorous medical tests to prove that they are entitled to it. Those judged capable of work will have to attend "work-focused interviews" and take part in "work-related activities". At these interviews employment advisers will be available to help place people in appropriate employment. Claimants who refuse to attend for interview will have their payments cut. Those who take up employment will qualify for extra benefits. The practice of increasing benefits over time will be scrapped.

The UK already spends a greater percentage of its Gross Domestic Product (GDP) on schemes for disabled workers than any other country in the European Union. We are determined to continue to move people from welfare into work. Our proposed reform should lead to a million fewer Incapacity Benefit claimants by 2016. The social and economic benefits of work to the individual are obvious. New technology ensures that work is now less physically demanding. Savings made from the reform of Incapacity Benefit will, of course, be welcome. However, our main aim is to return to the fundamental principles of the welfare state. It is surely far better to help people into the workplace than to condemn them to a life on benefits!

Russell Barclay, Department for Work and Pensions (DWP) Spokesperson

SOURCE B: ESA WILL INCREASE HARDSHIP

In the UK today, more people than ever are in need of support from public funds. There are 7 million people of working age with either a mental or physical disability. Charities raise millions of pounds to plug the income and health gaps in the welfare state. They already spend more on the disabled than on any other group. Yet surely it is the responsibility of the state – not charities – to support people in need. There may well be 2·7 million who claim Incapacity Benefit but the number actually receiving Incapacity Benefit fell from 1·9 million in 1995 to 1·7 million in 2004, as so many claimants are turned down. This shows how tough the rules are already.

Politicians should not complain about the cost of the welfare state, and certainly never about Incapacity Benefit. During the 1980s, it was government policy to encourage people to claim Incapacity Benefit in order to hide the true level of unemployment. Now, the Government will increase hardship by discouraging people from claiming a benefit to which they should be entitled. Disability experts forecast big problems in deciding who is fit enough to work. Mistakes will be made. Many claimants will be unable to cope with the stress of attending interviews. Others will be pressed into taking and keeping jobs for which they are neither physically nor mentally fit. It is disgraceful that those with disabilities, and other groups vulnerable to poverty, such as lone-parents, are being forced into employment situations that they are unable to cope with. "Welfare to Work" policies are clearly more about saving money than meeting needs.

We live in an unequal society where there are obstacles to employment for many disabled people. Around a million people who want to work cannot find jobs, as employers are reluctant to take on staff with disabilities or other health problems. UK Government spending on the sick and disabled is already lower than for any other group and a lower percentage of one-parent families receive Incapacity/Disability Benefit than any other benefit. Effective laws to prevent discrimination against the disabled would be far more useful than making the rules for Incapacity Benefit even tougher. We fully support any proposals that help disabled people to get jobs but we totally oppose this proposed reform of Incapacity Benefit. An Employment and Support Allowance (ESA) will only lead to more social exclusion and undermine the collectivist principles of the welfare state.

Irene Graham, Disability Support Group (DSG) Spokesperson

[Turn over for Source C on *Pages four* and *five*

SOURCE C: STATISTICAL INFORMATION

SOURCE C1: Reasons given by people of working age for not working

Male %	Reasons	Female %
37	Long-term sickness/disability	21
6	Looking after family/home	45
30	Student	19
13	Early retirement	4
14	Other	11

Source: Adapted from Labour Force Survey, Office for National Statistics

SOURCE C2:

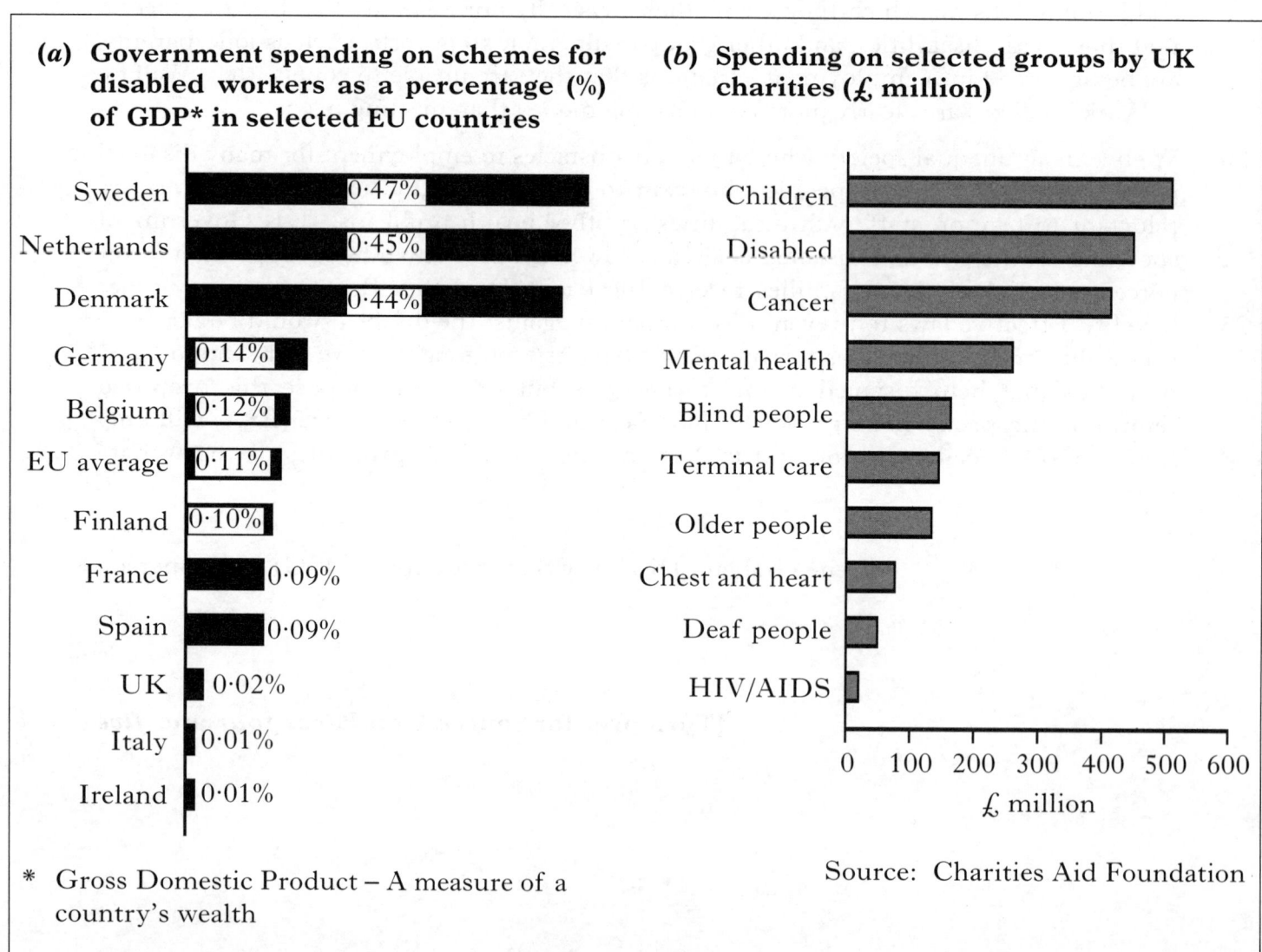

(a) Government spending on schemes for disabled workers as a percentage (%) of GDP* in selected EU countries

Country	%
Sweden	0·47%
Netherlands	0·45%
Denmark	0·44%
Germany	0·14%
Belgium	0·12%
EU average	0·11%
Finland	0·10%
France	0·09%
Spain	0·09%
UK	0·02%
Italy	0·01%
Ireland	0·01%

(b) Spending on selected groups by UK charities (£ million)

* Gross Domestic Product – A measure of a country's wealth

Source: Charities Aid Foundation

SOURCE C: (CONTINUED)

SOURCE C3:

(a) Percentage (%) share, by group, of UK Government benefit spending

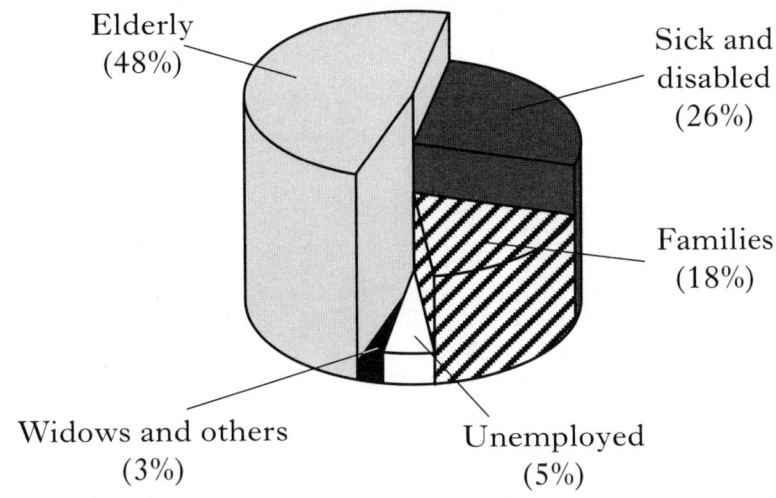

Elderly (48%)
Sick and disabled (26%)
Families (18%)
Widows and others (3%)
Unemployed (5%)

Source: Adapted from Department for Work and Pensions

(b) Percentage (%) of one-parent families receiving selected benefits

Benefit	(%)
Child	97
Working Families Tax Credit, Income Support **or** Minimum Income Guarantee	76
Incapacity/Disability	9
Council Tax	49
Housing	48

Source: Adapted from Family Resources Survey, Department for Work and Pensions

[BLANK PAGE]

DECISION MAKING EXERCISE

QUESTIONS

Marks

Questions 1 to 3 are based on Sources A to C on pages 2–5. Answer Questions 1 to 3 before attempting Question 4.

In Questions 1 to 3, use **only** the Sources described in each question.

Question 1 Use **only** *Source C1 and Source A.*

To what extent does the evidence support Russell Barclay? 3

Question 2

(a) Use **only** *Source C2(a) and Source A.*

Why might Russell Barclay be accused of exaggeration? 2

(b) Use **only** *Source C2(b) and Source B.*

Why might Irene Graham be accused of exaggeration? 2

Question 3 Use **only** *Source C3(a), Source C3(b) and Source B.*

To what extent does the evidence support Irene Graham? 3

(10)

Question 4

Marks

DECISION MAKING TASK

You are a social policy researcher. You have been asked to prepare a report for a committee investigating welfare provision in which you recommend or reject the proposal to introduce an Employment and Support Allowance (ESA).

Your answer should be written in a style appropriate to a *report*.

Your report should:

- recommend or reject the proposal to introduce an Employment and Support Allowance (ESA)
- provide arguments to support your decision
- identify and comment on any arguments which may be presented by those who oppose your decision
- refer to all the Sources provided

  AND

- **must** include relevant background knowledge.

The written and statistical sources which have been provided are:

SOURCE A: ESA will be fairer
SOURCE B: ESA will increase hardship
SOURCE C: Statistical Information

(20)

Total: 30 Marks

[END OF QUESTION PAPER]

HIGHER
2008

X236/301

NATIONAL
QUALIFICATIONS
2008

THURSDAY, 29 MAY
9.00 AM – 10.30 AM

MODERN STUDIES
HIGHER
Paper 1

Candidates should answer **FOUR** questions:

- **ONE** from Section A

and

- **ONE** from Section B

and

- **ONE** from Section C

and

- **ONE OTHER** from **EITHER** Section A **OR** Section C

Section A: Political Issues in the United Kingdom.
Section B: Social Issues in the United Kingdom.
Section C: International Issues.

Each question is worth 15 marks.

PB X236/301 6/13370

SECTION A—Political Issues in the United Kingdom

Each question is worth 15 marks

STUDY THEME 1A: DEVOLVED DECISION MAKING IN SCOTLAND

Question A1

Critically examine the role of local government in a devolved Scotland.

STUDY THEME 1B: DECISION MAKING IN CENTRAL GOVERNMENT

Question A2

Assess the effectiveness of pressure groups in influencing decision-making in Central Government.

STUDY THEME 1C: POLITICAL PARTIES AND THEIR POLICIES (INCLUDING THE SCOTTISH DIMENSION)

Question A3

There are few policy differences between the main political parties.
Discuss.

STUDY THEME 1D: ELECTORAL SYSTEMS, VOTING AND POLITICAL ATTITUDES

Question A4

Assess the influence of social class on voting behaviour.

SECTION B — Social Issues in the United Kingdom

Each question is worth 15 marks

STUDY THEME 2: WEALTH AND HEALTH INEQUALITIES IN THE UNITED KINGDOM

EITHER

Question B5

Assess the effectiveness of government policies to reduce gender and ethnic inequalities.

OR

Question B6

Critically examine the view that government, not individuals, should be responsible for health care and welfare provision.

[Turn over

SECTION C — International Issues
Each question is worth 15 marks

STUDY THEME 3A: THE REPUBLIC OF SOUTH AFRICA

Question C7

Assess the effectiveness of Black Economic Empowerment in reducing inequalities.

STUDY THEME 3B: THE PEOPLE'S REPUBLIC OF CHINA

Question C8

Critically examine the view that China is becoming a more democratic society.

STUDY THEME 3C: THE UNITED STATES OF AMERICA

Question C9

Assess the effectiveness of Congress and the Supreme Court in checking the powers of the President.

STUDY THEME 3D: THE EUROPEAN UNION

Question C10

Assess the impact of enlargement on the European Union.

STUDY THEME 3E: THE POLITICS OF DEVELOPMENT IN AFRICA

Question C11

With reference to specific African countries (excluding the Republic of South Africa):

Assess the importance of education and health care to successful development.

STUDY THEME 3F: GLOBAL SECURITY

Question C12

Critically examine the part played by the USA in achieving global security.

[END OF QUESTION PAPER]

X236/302

NATIONAL QUALIFICATIONS 2008

THURSDAY, 29 MAY 10.50 AM – 12.05 PM

MODERN STUDIES HIGHER
Paper 2

Summary of Decision Making Exercise

You are an expert on social policy. You have been asked to prepare a report for an all-party group of MSPs, in which you recommend or reject the proposal to make all prescriptions free in Scotland.

Before beginning the task, you must answer a number of evaluating questions (Questions 1–3) based on the source material provided. The source material is:

SOURCE A: Prescription Charges are a Danger to Health

SOURCE B: Prescription Charges are Necessary

SOURCE C: Statistical Information

SOURCE A: PRESCRIPTION CHARGES ARE A DANGER TO HEALTH

The Scottish Government is to be commended for its determination to phase out and eventually abolish prescription charges. Since first introduced, prescription charges have been kept ever since, except for a brief period of abolition in the 1960s. Although large numbers of prescriptions are dispensed free, the price per item is such that many adults find it very difficult to pay.

Since April 2007, all patients registered with a Welsh GP, who get their prescriptions from a Welsh pharmacist, have been entitled to free prescriptions. There is no evidence that this has led to an increased demand for prescriptions in Wales. The suggestion that people ask for unnecessary prescriptions is ridiculous. The most common reasons for not handing in a prescription are to do with cost—no one finds that they did not need it after all. Prescription charges prevent the sick from getting essential medicines. Being forced to decide which item on a prescription they can afford is one choice that patients can do without. The effects of this on individuals, and in the longer term on the National Health Service (NHS), should be obvious! Interrupting or delaying treatment for just a few days can increase the risks to one's health. The long-term costs to the NHS become much greater because hospital treatment that could have been avoided becomes necessary. GPs have become so concerned about the consequences of prescription charges that one in five has admitted to falsifying paperwork to ensure that vulnerable patients get free prescriptions.

The prescription charge is a tax on the sick and not at all in keeping with the founding principles of the NHS. Furthermore, it undermines any attempts to tackle the health divide in a society in which the link between deprivation and ill health has been clearly established. The pre-payment certificate only benefits those who can afford it. There is no way that patients on low incomes can afford to pay the required lump sum in advance. The actual revenue gained from prescription charges is a tiny proportion of the estimated £10 billion budget for the NHS in Scotland. Making all prescriptions free in Scotland would be straightforward, effective and fair. Free prescriptions would make a huge difference as to whether people would or would not go to a doctor. There would be an immediate improvement in the health of the nation from which future generations would only benefit.

Daphne Millar, Anti-Poverty Campaigner

SOURCE B: PRESCRIPTION CHARGES ARE NECESSARY

Within a few years of the creation of the NHS, a charge for each item on a prescription was introduced in response to the rising costs of medicines. However, children under 16 and men and women aged 60 and over get free prescriptions. Other categories of people are also entitled to exemption from NHS prescription charges. Around half of the population qualify for free prescriptions. This results in 90% of dispensed prescription items being issued free of charge. For those who do have to pay, there is a system of pre-payment certificates. This gives unlimited prescriptions for up to twelve months for a one-off payment. Furthermore, almost two in every three medicines available on prescription can be bought more cheaply over the counter. Despite prescription charges, the NHS has always enjoyed strong public support. In a recent survey on health care systems in European countries, the UK was one of the highest rated.

The UK Government intends to keep prescription charges in England. The Scottish Government must keep them too. It is estimated that in the financial year 2007–2008, prescription charges brought in a much-needed £46 million in revenue to the NHS in Scotland. Such a sum buys a lot of health care, be it equipment or staff. Abolish charges, and the demand for unnecessary prescriptions will surely increase. GPs are concerned about the number of patients who consult them for no good medical reason. If charges are abolished, the number of patients asking doctors for unnecessary prescriptions will increase. This will put pressure on the drugs budget and may mean delays in introducing life saving but expensive new drugs.

Abolishing prescription charges will not help those on low incomes. It will divert resources towards those on middle and upper incomes. Most people who have to pay can afford all of the items on their prescriptions and there is little support from health and community groups for completely abolishing prescription charges. Abolishing prescription charges would have a bad effect on both the financing and performance of the NHS in Scotland. The resulting cutbacks in the provision of care would hit the poorest members of society the most. Prescription charges must be retained if the health gap is to be closed.

Tom Beattie, Health Economist

[Turn over for Source C on *Pages four* and *five*

SOURCE C: STATISTICAL INFORMATION

SOURCE C1: Public opinion survey results

(a) Reasons patients gave for not handing in prescriptions

It cost less to buy the medicine over the counter	28%
It cost too much money (£6·85 per item)	25%
Health improved – did not need it after all	10%
I wanted to wait and see if I felt better	16%
I didn't feel I was prescribed the correct medicine	11%
I had some medicine left from the last time	5%
I forgot about it	5%

Source: Adapted from Consultation on Review of NHS Prescription Charges (Scotland) 2007

(b) If all prescriptions became free, in what way would it influence your decision to go to the doctor?

% of people surveyed

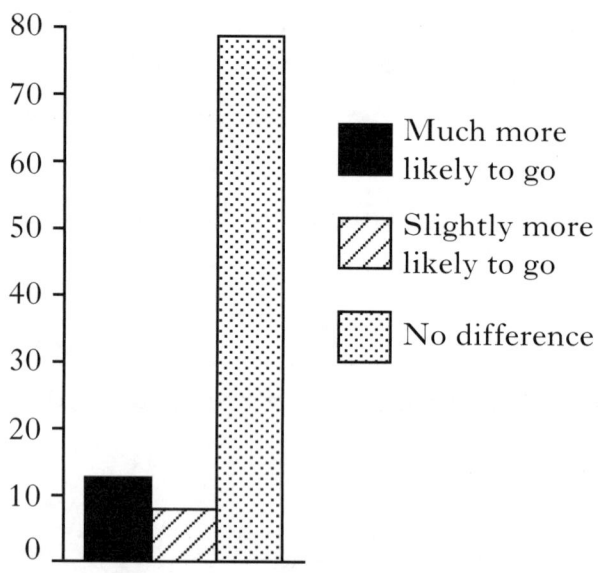

Source: Adapted from Consultation on Review of NHS Prescription Charges (Scotland) 2007

(c) In the past year, how many items on your prescriptions have you been able to afford?

% of people surveyed

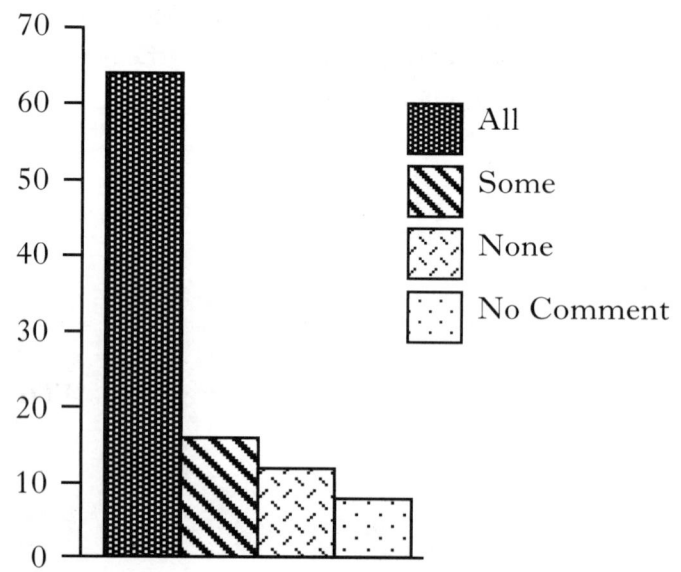

Source: Adapted from National Association of Citizens Advice Bureaux data 2001

SOURCE C: **(CONTINUED)**

SOURCE C2: How people rate their health care systems (perfect score 100)

Country	Score
Belgium	66
France	65
Germany	76
Hungary	58
Italy	48
Netherlands	80
Poland	41
Spain	61
Sweden	66
Switzerland	78
UK	60

Source: Adapted from *The Times*, June 2005

SOURCE C3: Results of consultation with health and community groups

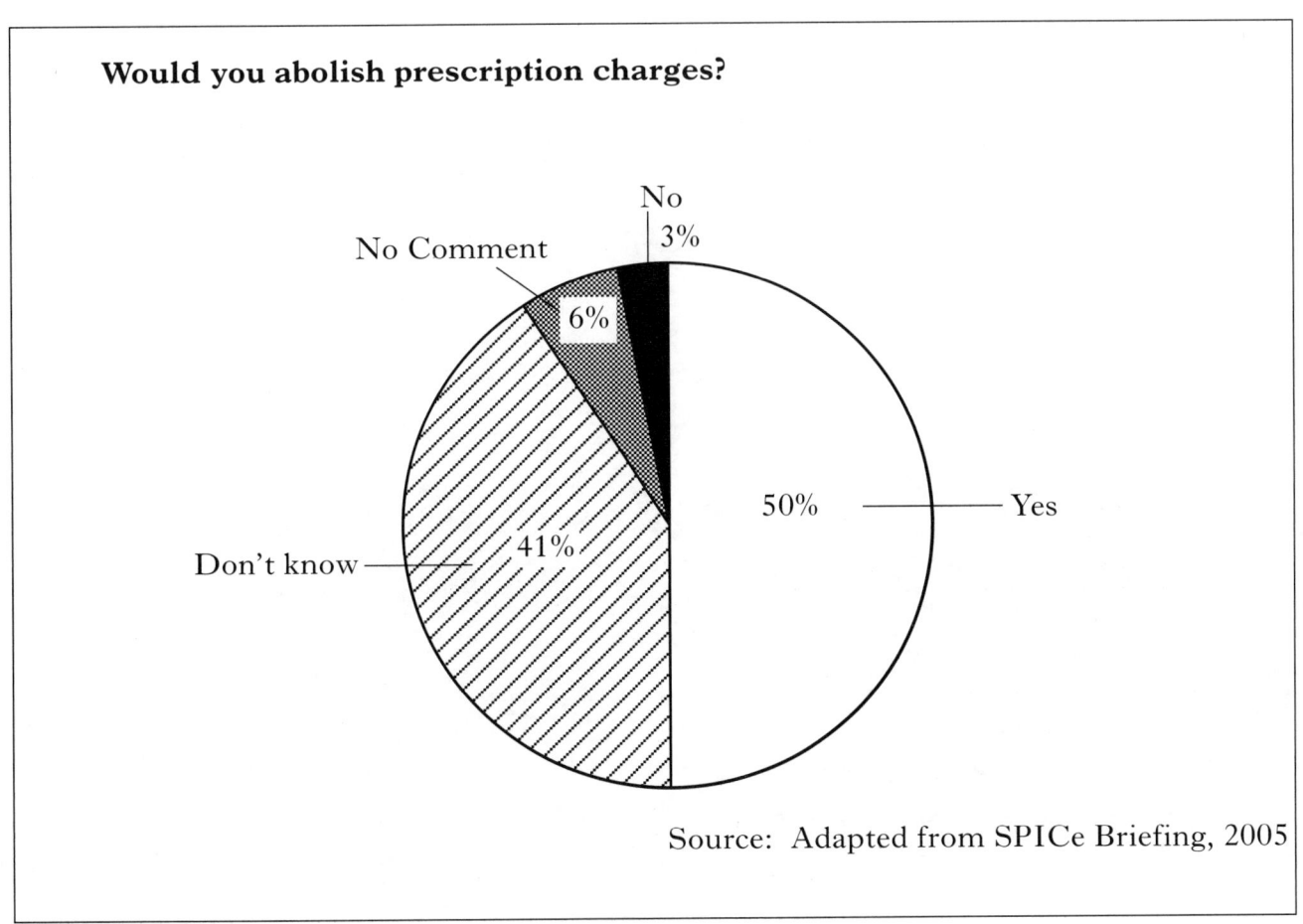

Source: Adapted from SPICe Briefing, 2005

[BLANK PAGE]

DECISION MAKING EXERCISE

QUESTIONS Marks

Questions 1 to 3 are based on Sources A to C on pages 2–5. Answer Questions 1 to 3 before attempting Question 4.

In Questions 1 to 3, use **only** the Sources described in each question.

Question 1   Use **only** Source C1(a) and Source A.

To what extent does the evidence support Daphne Millar?   3

Question 2

(a) Use **only** Source C1(b) and Source A.

Why might Daphne Millar be accused of exaggeration?   2

(b) Use **only** Source C2 and Source B.

Why might Tom Beattie be accused of exaggeration?   2

Question 3   Use **only** Source C1(c) and Source C3 and Source B.

To what extent does the evidence support Tom Beattie?   3

(10)

Question 4 Marks

DECISION MAKING TASK

You are an expert on social policy. You have been asked to prepare a report for an all-party group of MSPs, in which you recommend or reject the proposal to make all prescriptions free in Scotland.

Your answer should be written in a style of a *report*.

Your report should:

- recommend or reject the proposal to make all prescriptions free in Scotland
- provide arguments to support your decision
- identify and comment on any arguments which may be presented by those who oppose your decision
- refer to all the Sources provided

  AND

- **must** include relevant background knowledge.

The written and statistical sources which have been provided are:

SOURCE A: Prescription Charges are a Danger to Health
SOURCE B: Prescription Charges are Necessary
SOURCE C: Statistical Information

(20)

Total: 30 Marks

[END OF QUESTION PAPER]

HIGHER

2009

X236/301

NATIONAL QUALIFICATIONS 2009

MONDAY, 25 MAY 9.00 AM – 10.30 AM

MODERN STUDIES HIGHER
Paper 1

Candidates should answer **FOUR** questions:

- **ONE** from Section A

and

- **ONE** from Section B

and

- **ONE** from Section C

and

- **ONE OTHER** from **EITHER** Section A **OR** Section C

Section A: Political Issues in the United Kingdom.
Section B: Social Issues in the United Kingdom.
Section C: International Issues.

Each question is worth 15 marks.

SECTION A—Political Issues in the United Kingdom
Each question is worth 15 marks

STUDY THEME 1A: DEVOLVED DECISION MAKING IN SCOTLAND

Question A1

Assess the impact of devolution on decision making for Scotland.

STUDY THEME 1B: DECISION MAKING IN CENTRAL GOVERNMENT

Question A2

Backbench MPs have little influence on decision making in Central Government.
Discuss.

STUDY THEME 1C: POLITICAL PARTIES AND THEIR POLICIES (INCLUDING THE SCOTTISH DIMENSION)

Question A3

To what extent are there ideological differences within and between the main political parties?

STUDY THEME 1D: ELECTORAL SYSTEMS, VOTING AND POLITICAL ATTITUDES

Question A4

Critically examine the view that the media is the most important influence on voting behaviour.

SECTION B — Social Issues in the United Kingdom

Each question is worth 15 marks

STUDY THEME 2: WEALTH AND HEALTH INEQUALITIES IN THE UNITED KINGDOM

EITHER

Question B5

Assess the impact of income on health.

OR

Question B6

Critically examine the success of recent government policies to reduce poverty.

[Turn over for Section C on *Page four*

SECTION C — International Issues
Each question is worth 15 marks

STUDY THEME 3A: THE REPUBLIC OF SOUTH AFRICA

Question C7

Critically examine the view that inequalities exist only *between* different racial groups.

STUDY THEME 3B: THE PEOPLE'S REPUBLIC OF CHINA

Question C8

Critically examine the view that there is little demand for political reform because of greater social and economic freedom.

STUDY THEME 3C: THE UNITED STATES OF AMERICA

Question C9

To what extent do ethnic minorities achieve the American Dream?

STUDY THEME 3D: THE EUROPEAN UNION

Question C10

The Council of Ministers is the most important decision-making institution in the EU.
Discuss.

STUDY THEME 3E: THE POLITICS OF DEVELOPMENT IN AFRICA

Question C11

With reference to specific African countries (excluding the Republic of South Africa):

Assess the influence of Non Governmental Organisations on development.

STUDY THEME 3F: GLOBAL SECURITY

Question C12

Assess the effectiveness of the United Nations in dealing with threats to international peace and security.

[END OF QUESTION PAPER]

X236/302

NATIONAL
QUALIFICATIONS
2009

MONDAY, 25 MAY
10.50 AM – 12.05 PM

MODERN STUDIES
HIGHER
Paper 2

Summary of Decision Making Exercise

You are a policy researcher in the Department for Work and Pensions. You have been asked to prepare a report in which you recommend or reject Fifty-Fifty, a proposal that women hold the same number of senior management posts in the public services as men.

Before beginning the task, you must answer a number of evaluating questions (Questions 1–3) based on the source material provided. The source material is:

SOURCE A: Fifty-Fifty will deliver equality

SOURCE B: Fifty-Fifty is not the solution

SOURCE C: Statistical Information

SOURCE A: FIFTY-FIFTY WILL DELIVER EQUALITY

The glass ceiling in the UK has proved to be very robust. Many women who choose a career path in the public services are being prevented from reaching their full potential both personally and economically. This is a waste of their talents, the money spent on their training, and a severe loss to the UK economy as a whole.

Fifty-Fifty will make it compulsory for women to hold the same number of senior management posts in the public services as men. Public services will be required to set out strategies on how they will meet this target. The percentage of women in senior positions in the public services is well below that of men, so it comes as no surprise that the UK has the largest gender pay gap in the European Union. The fact that in 2007 male staff at St Andrews University earned, on average, 23% more than their female colleagues is only one of the many examples of unequal pay to be found in the UK.

Government has a responsibility to promote equal opportunities. Yet despite over thirty years of legislation, the UK still does not have gender equality. All too often the approach of government has been to recognise that things are unfair, acknowledge that "something" should be done, then ignore any advice it receives. The Women and Work Commission (2004–2006) made forty recommendations. One of these was that girls be encouraged to consider work other than catering, clerical and the rest of the "Five Cs". Even now, there is concern that many schools still stereotype girls when it comes to work experience and careers guidance.

Surely no one can dispute the reasons why Fifty-Fifty is necessary. We have no shortage of talented female staff in our public services. Filling posts will not be a problem. Fifty-Fifty will mean that women will be guaranteed their fair share of senior appointments. This will end gender segregation in, and bring fresh approaches to, the delivery of public services. Well over half of women say that having children is the biggest obstacle they face in pursuing a successful career. For many women, motherhood effectively ends their chance of promotion. The gap between male and female opportunities and rewards is unacceptable and the current pace of progress towards equality does little for the UK's equal opportunities record. Fifty-Fifty is a practical and effective solution to a centuries old problem: the glass ceiling will be smashed once and for all.

Avril Beattie, Equal Opportunities Spokesperson

SOURCE B: FIFTY-FIFTY IS NOT THE SOLUTION

Fifty-Fifty is not the solution to gender inequalities in employment. Gender is irrelevant to a person's ability to do the job. We must never depart from the principle that senior management posts should go to the best person for the job. In any case, change is already taking place. More girls than boys are going into both full time higher/further education and employment. It is only a matter of time before these high achieving girls go on to occupy top managerial posts at the expense of males.

Government has already recognised that words alone are not enough and that action must be taken to address gender inequalities. There has been a great deal of gender equality legislation in recent years. In addition, diversity targets have been set for the Civil Service. We have reached a point where equality laws are actually holding back women's careers.

It should not be up to government to decide who makes it to the top posts in management. Surely it is a matter of individual choice and responsibility. There are plenty of high profile women who have achieved great success in a wide range of careers. The Fifty-Fifty proposal is an insult to these high achievers. It is patronising to female staff to say that they are not good enough to get promotion on their own merits. Fifty-Fifty will only increase the time already being spent on tracking and monitoring. It will become more difficult to both recruit and retain high quality male staff. Many talented men will leave for better opportunities in the private sector. What our public services need are more resources to tackle the UK's many social problems. Tackling these should be the priority for the public services, not the expense of chasing politically correct gender targets.

The UK has an excellent equal opportunities record with one of the highest percentages of women in senior management in the world. In any case, not all women want to reach the dizzy heights of senior management—and the added pressure it brings. Many women have recognised the importance of a healthy work-life balance and made an informed decision to choose family life before a career. The overall gap in weekly earnings between male and female workers is tiny. Fifty-Fifty will only improve opportunities for those at the top and is by no means the solution to wider inequalities in society.

Jim Waugh, Businessman

[Turn over for Source C on *Pages four* and *five*

SOURCE C: STATISTICAL INFORMATION

SOURCE C1 (a) Women in public service senior management in the UK, 2005 (%)

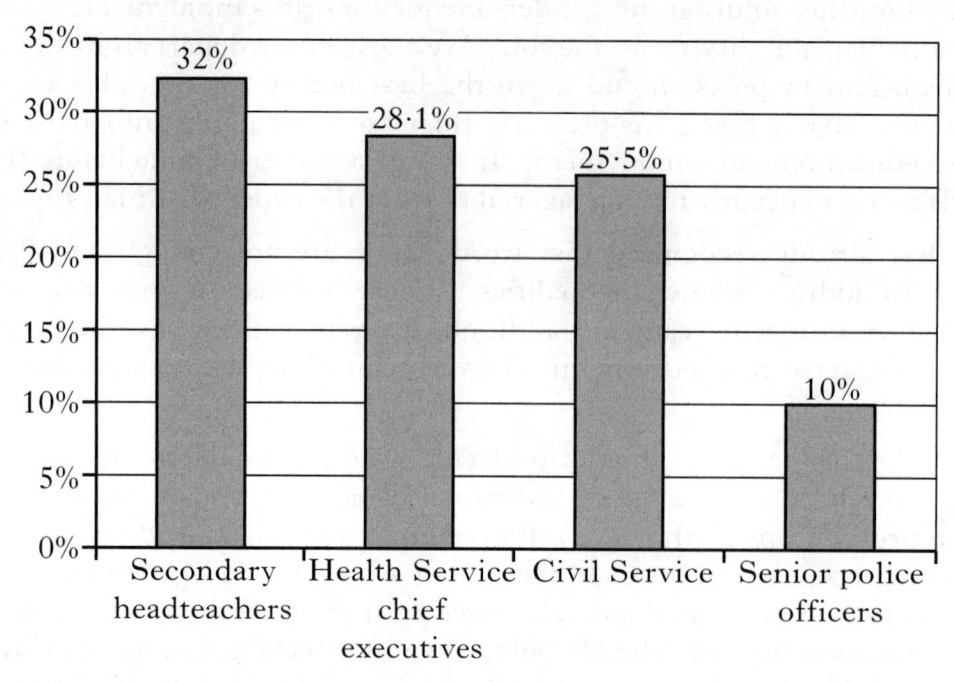

Category	Percentage
Secondary headteachers	32%
Health Service chief executives	28·1%
Civil Service	25·5%
Senior police officers	10%

SOURCE C1 (b) Gender pay gap in the EU, 2005 (%)

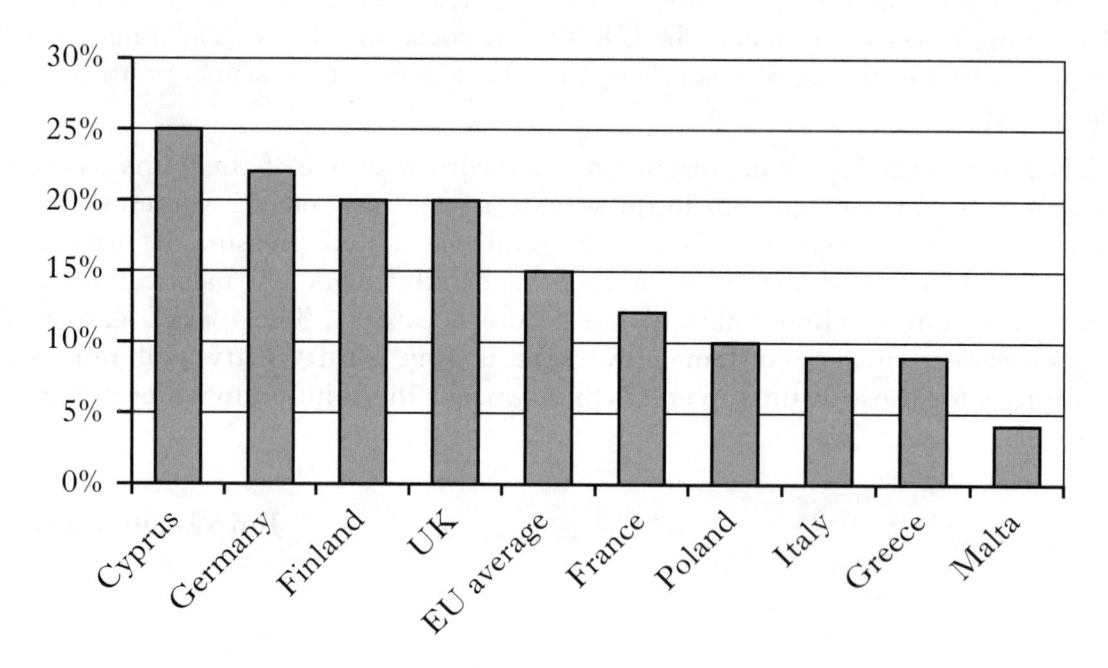

Country	Percentage
Cyprus	25%
Germany	22%
Finland	20%
UK	20%
EU average	15%
France	12%
Poland	10%
Italy	9%
Greece	9%
Malta	4%

SOURCE C2 (a) Female public opinion survey

What is the biggest obstacle you face in pursuing a successful career?

Bad/inconsiderate attitudes in the workplace	44%
Having children	48%
Nothing: women have equal opportunities	8%

SOURCE C: (CONTINUED)

SOURCE C2 (b) Percentage of school leavers from state schools in Scotland by destination and gender, 2006–2007

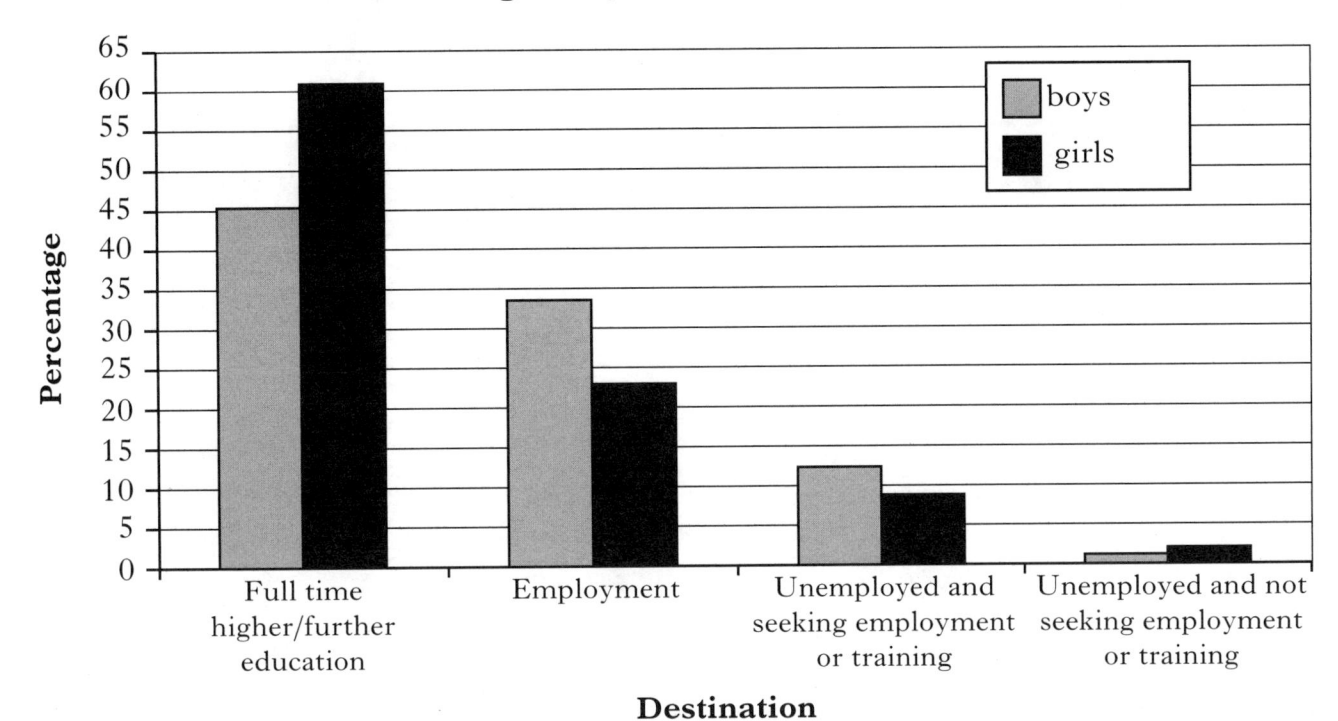

Destination	Boys (%)	Girls (%)
Full time higher/further education	45	61
Employment	34	23
Unemployed and seeking employment or training	13	9
Unemployed and not seeking employment or training	2	3

SOURCE C3 Senior management posts occupied by women in selected countries, 2006 (%)

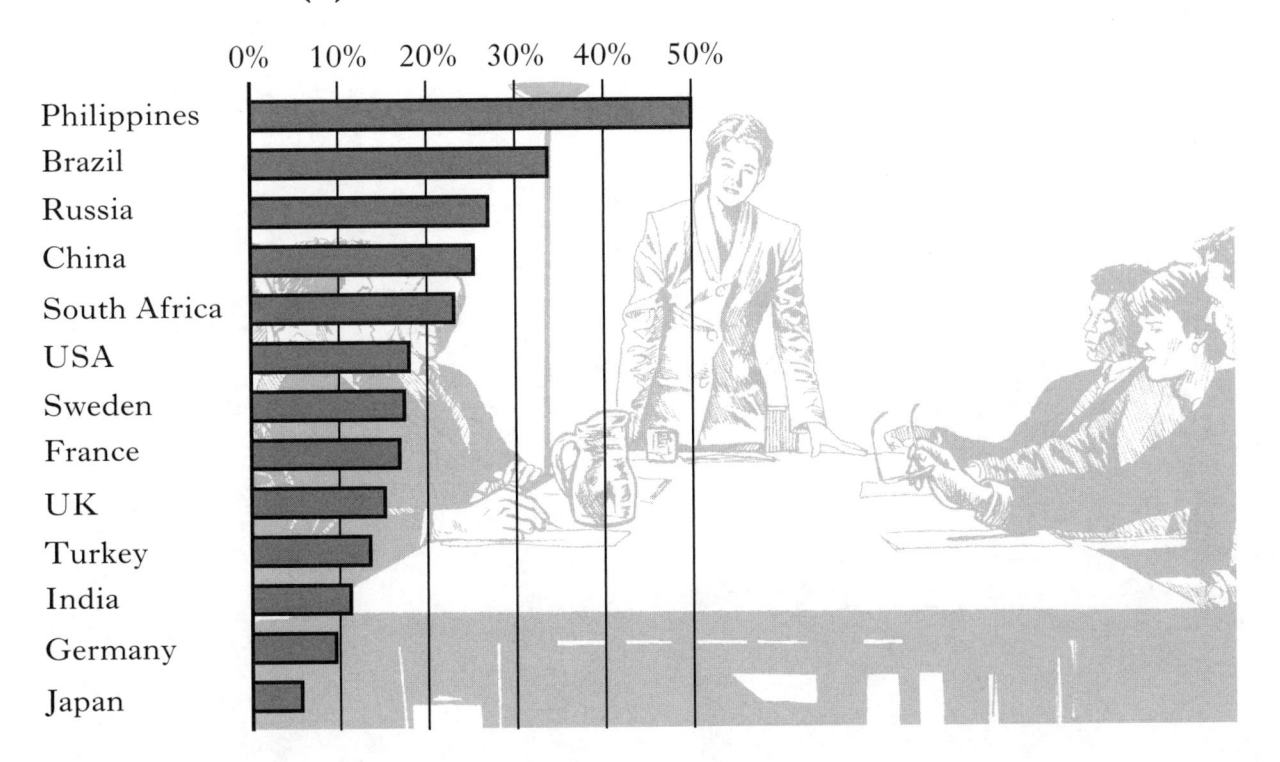

Country	%
Philippines	50
Brazil	35
Russia	28
China	26
South Africa	24
USA	22
Sweden	22
France	21
UK	19
Turkey	17
India	15
Germany	12
Japan	7

DECISION MAKING EXERCISE

QUESTIONS

Marks

Questions 1 to 3 are based on Sources A to C on pages 2–5. Answer Questions 1 to 3 before attempting Question 4.

In Questions 1 to 3, use <u>only</u> the Sources described in each question.

Question 1 Use **only** *Source C1(a), Source C1(b) and Source A*.

To what extent does the evidence support the view of Avril Beattie?   3

Question 2

(a) Use **only** *Source C2(a) and Source A*.

    Why might Avril Beattie be accused of exaggeration?   2

(b) Use **only** *Source C2(b) and Source B*.

    To what extent does the evidence support the view of Jim Waugh?   3

Question 3 Use **only** *Source C3 and Source B*.

Why might Jim Waugh be accused of exaggeration?   2

    (10)

[X236/302]   *Page one (Insert)*

Question 4

Marks

DECISION MAKING TASK

You are a policy researcher in the Department for Work and Pensions. You have been asked to prepare a report in which you recommend or reject Fifty-Fifty, a proposal that women hold the same number of senior management posts in the public services as men.

Your answer should be written in the style of a *report*.

Your report should:

- recommend or reject Fifty-Fifty
- provide arguments to support your decision
- identify and comment on any arguments which may be presented by those who oppose your decision
- refer to all the Sources provided

    AND

- **must** include relevant background knowledge.

The written and statistical sources which are provided are:

SOURCE A: Fifty-Fifty will deliver equality

SOURCE B: Fifty-Fifty is not the solution

SOURCE C: Statistical Information

(20)

Total: 30 Marks

[END OF QUESTION PAPER]

HIGHER

2010

X236/301

NATIONAL QUALIFICATIONS 2010

TUESDAY, 25 MAY 9.00 AM – 10.30 AM

MODERN STUDIES HIGHER
Paper 1

Candidates should answer **FOUR** questions:

- **ONE** from Section A

and

- **ONE** from Section B

and

- **ONE** from Section C

and

ONE OTHER from **EITHER** Section A **OR** Section C

Section A: Political Issues in the United Kingdom
Section B: Social Issues in the United Kingdom
Section C: International Issues.

Each question is worth 15 marks.

SECTION A—Political Issues in the United Kingdom

Each question is worth 15 marks

STUDY THEME 1A: DEVOLVED DECISION MAKING IN SCOTLAND

Question A1

With devolution there is no need for Scottish representation at Westminster.
Discuss.

STUDY THEME 1B: DECISION MAKING IN CENTRAL GOVERNMENT

Question A2

Critically examine the view that the UK Parliament has little control over the Executive.

STUDY THEME 1C: POLITICAL PARTIES AND THEIR POLICIES (INCLUDING THE SCOTTISH DIMENSION)

Question A3

To what extent do party members decide their party's policies?

STUDY THEME 1D: ELECTORAL SYSTEMS, VOTING AND POLITICAL ATTITUDES

Question A4

The Single Transferable Vote electoral system provides for better representation than First Past the Post.
Discuss.

SECTION B — Social Issues in the United Kingdom

Each question is worth 15 marks

STUDY THEME 2: WEALTH AND HEALTH INEQUALITIES IN THE UNITED KINGDOM

EITHER

Question B5

Individual lifestyle choices limit good health more than any other factor.
Discuss.

OR

Question B6

To what extent have government policies reduced gender **and/or** ethnic inequalities?

[Turn over for Section C on *Page four*

SECTION C — International Issues
Each question is worth 15 marks

STUDY THEME 3A: THE REPUBLIC OF SOUTH AFRICA

Question C7

To what extent is South Africa a multi-party democracy?

STUDY THEME 3B: THE PEOPLE'S REPUBLIC OF CHINA

Question C8

Critically examine the view that there is little opposition to the Communist Party in China.

STUDY THEME 3C: THE UNITED STATES OF AMERICA

Question C9

Assess the impact of recent immigration on the USA.

STUDY THEME 3D: THE EUROPEAN UNION

Question C10

Critically examine the view that the Common Agricultural and Fisheries Policies have benefited the member states of the European Union.

STUDY THEME 3E: THE POLITICS OF DEVELOPMENT IN AFRICA

Question C11

With reference to specific African countries (excluding the Republic of South Africa):

The United Nations Organisation (UNO) has been effective in promoting development.
Discuss.

STUDY THEME 3F: GLOBAL SECURITY

Question C12

Assess the effectiveness of NATO in achieving international peace and security.

[END OF QUESTION PAPER]

X236/302

NATIONAL
QUALIFICATIONS
2010

TUESDAY, 25 MAY
10.50 AM – 12.05 PM

MODERN STUDIES
HIGHER
Paper 2

Summary of Decision Making Exercise

You are a health policy adviser. You have been asked to prepare a report for the Scottish Government Cabinet Secretary for Health and Wellbeing in which you recommend or reject a proposal to introduce Well Man Clinics to every part of Scotland.

Before beginning the task, you must answer a number of evaluating questions (Questions 1–3) based on the source material provided. The source material is:

SOURCE A: Well Man Clinics are an Urgent Priority

SOURCE B: Well Man Clinics are a Waste of Resources

SOURCE C: Statistical Information

SOURCE A: WELL MAN CLINICS ARE AN URGENT PRIORITY

Numerous reports prove that the health of men in this country is worse than the health of women. Urgent Government action to close the gender health gap is required. Year after year, male death rates are higher than female death rates for all causes and men have lower life expectancy across Scotland. While attention has, in the past, been focused on improving women's health, recent equality legislation now demands that all groups receive equal access to health advice and health care services. Therefore, one immediate and practical response to reduce the gender health gap must be to expand the number of Well Man Clinics to every part of Scotland.

Well Man Clinics are appointment-free, drop-in facilities where men can choose to receive expert health advice on a range of health matters such as diet and fitness or on those issues particular only to males. Any man voluntarily attending would have the opportunity to speak to a dedicated health professional and the advice offered would be given in a supportive and non-judgemental way. In some parts of Scotland, Well Man Clinics have already been piloted. So far these appear to have worked well. Initial reviews show that the opening of Well Man Clinics has been welcomed by men. Establishing Well Man Clinics in the rest of Scotland would have a significant impact on reducing male ill-health. For a relatively small NHS investment there would be enormous long-term financial savings. Prevention is always better than cure.

Well Man Clinics would work alongside the many educational health campaigns already being run by the Scottish Government. These clinics will offer men positive choices in life. This is not a case of government lecturing men to live healthier lives. As things stand, there is a need to encourage men to consider their own health. Men are not making full use of traditional GP services. Health studies indicate that most men want to live healthier lifestyles but they need advice and support within their communities to enable this to happen. Studies show that too many men are making the wrong lifestyle choices. They continue to smoke, they fail to take enough exercise or they eat a poor diet. Recent figures on alcohol consumption make uncomfortable reading. Annually, the number of males exceeding the recommended alcohol intake guidelines continues to increase.

Everyone knows there is no "quick fix" to improving men's health. Well Man Clinics would be just one part of a wider approach to health care that looks at tackling the various causes of Scotland's poor health. However, targeted intervention at the men who are most at risk does work. Well Man Clinics should be set up in all areas of Scotland.

Karen MacDonald, University Lecturer

SOURCE B: WELL MAN CLINICS ARE A WASTE OF RESOURCES

Expanding the number of Well Man Clinics is not the correct approach to tackling Scotland's poor health record. Well Man Clinics will make no impact on those men who most need to change their lifestyles. The "nanny state" approach will make little or no impact on the group of men putting themselves at the greatest risk. Instead, it is the "worried well" who will attend. Well Man Clinics will be used, in the main, by health-conscious, middle class professionals who already lead healthy lifestyles. There can be very few men who do not already know that smoking, alcohol, a lack of exercise or poor diet are bad for their health. In any event, more women now smoke than men in every age group. An increase in the number of male-only clinics targeting men's health will do nothing to reduce gender health inequality.

Instead of wasting scarce NHS resources on expanding the number of Well Man Clinics, the Scottish Government needs to address the underlying causes of social and economic inequality. For example, the link between poverty and poor health has been well documented. Priority must be given to policies that reduce poverty and not those that deal exclusively with male ill-health. There are already plenty of support agencies available to help those men who wish to lead healthier lifestyles. Resources allocated to expanding Well Man Clinics can only mean a reduction in services elsewhere in the NHS.

Well Man Clinics are well intentioned but they do not work. One evaluation of the pilot projects suggests that "one size does not fit all". Not all men want separate daytime health services for males. Surveys show most men wanted Well Man Clinics open in the evenings and a majority were unhappy with the information they received. Instead a variety of approaches to changing men's attitudes to their health is required. The previous Scottish Government spent £4 million on Well Man Clinics yet the success of these clinics has been, at best, mixed. This is in stark contrast to other health education programmes, such as those dealing with the use of illegal drugs, which have been far more successful. At a time when there are many competing demands on the NHS budget, £4 million does not represent best value in the use of taxpayers' money.

Tackling the health inequalities that exist in Scotland today requires something greater than what is offered by Well Man Clinics. In other countries where health inequalities have been successfully reduced a collectivist approach has been adopted. The Scottish Government, and the UK Government, have introduced some imaginative policies to improve health for all. Unfortunately, Well Man Clinics is not one of them.

William Walker, Anti-Poverty Campaigner

[Turn over for Source C on *Pages four, five* and *six*

SOURCE C: STATISTICAL INFORMATION

SOURCE C1 (a) Male and female death rates by selected causes in Scotland, 2003–2007 (per 100 000 population)

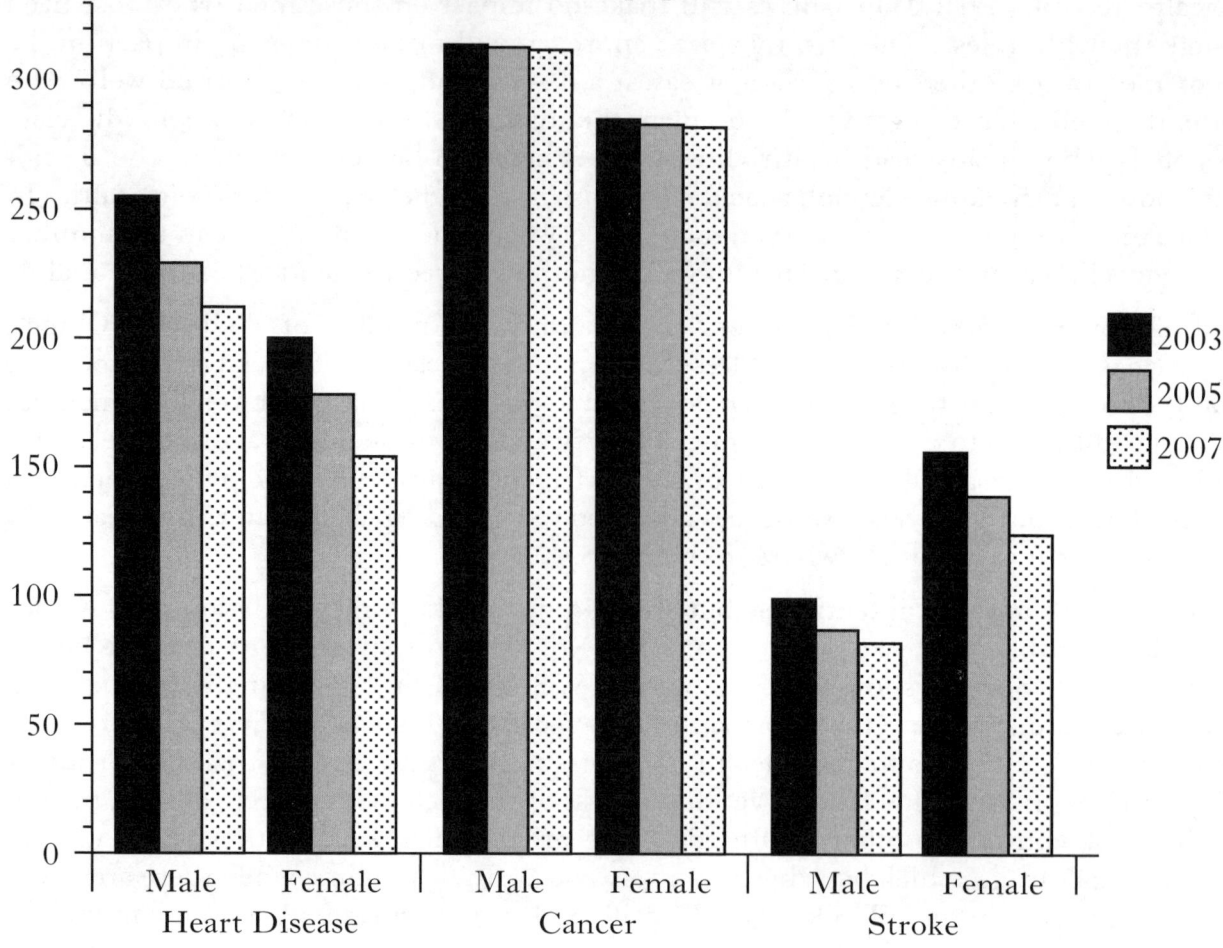

Legend: 2003, 2005, 2007

Heart Disease — Male: 2003 ~255, 2005 ~230, 2007 ~212; Female: 2003 ~200, 2005 ~178, 2007 ~154
Cancer — Male: 2003 ~313, 2005 ~312, 2007 ~310; Female: 2003 ~285, 2005 ~283, 2007 ~281
Stroke — Male: 2003 ~98, 2005 ~86, 2007 ~80; Female: 2003 ~156, 2005 ~138, 2007 ~122

SOURCE C1 (b) Male and female life expectancy at birth in Scotland, 2005 (by selected council area)

	Male	*Female*
Aberdeen City	75·0	79·9
Dundee City	73·0	78·4
East Ayrshire	73·7	78·0
East Renfrewshire	76·8	81·0
Glasgow City	69·9	76·7
Highland	75·0	80·3
Inverclyde	71·1	77·9
Perth and Kinross	76·4	80·6
Scottish Borders	75·8	80·0
West Dunbartonshire	71·0	77·5
All Scotland	**74·2**	**79·2**

Both Sources: Adapted from General Register Office for Scotland data

SOURCE C: (continued)

SOURCE C2 (a) **Percentage of Scottish adults exceeding recommended guidelines on alcohol intake: 1999–2005**

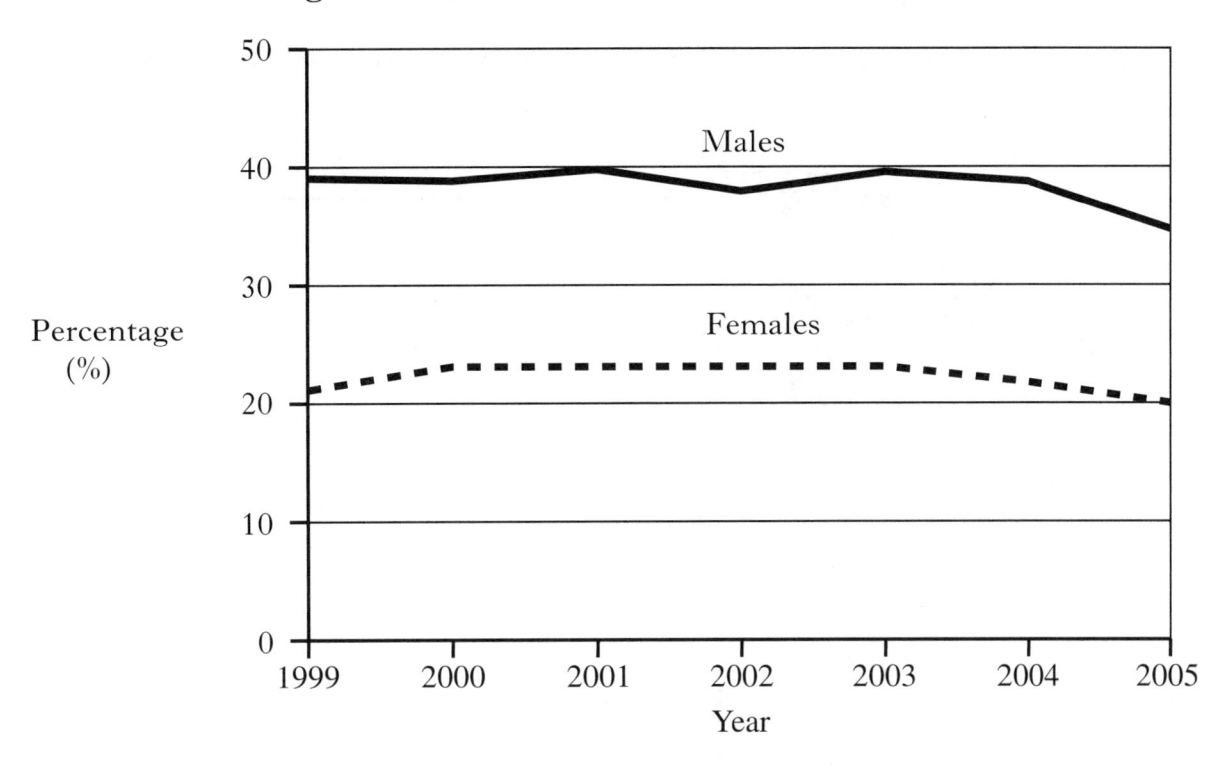

SOURCE C2 (b) **Percentage of Scottish adults who smoke; by age and sex (2005)**

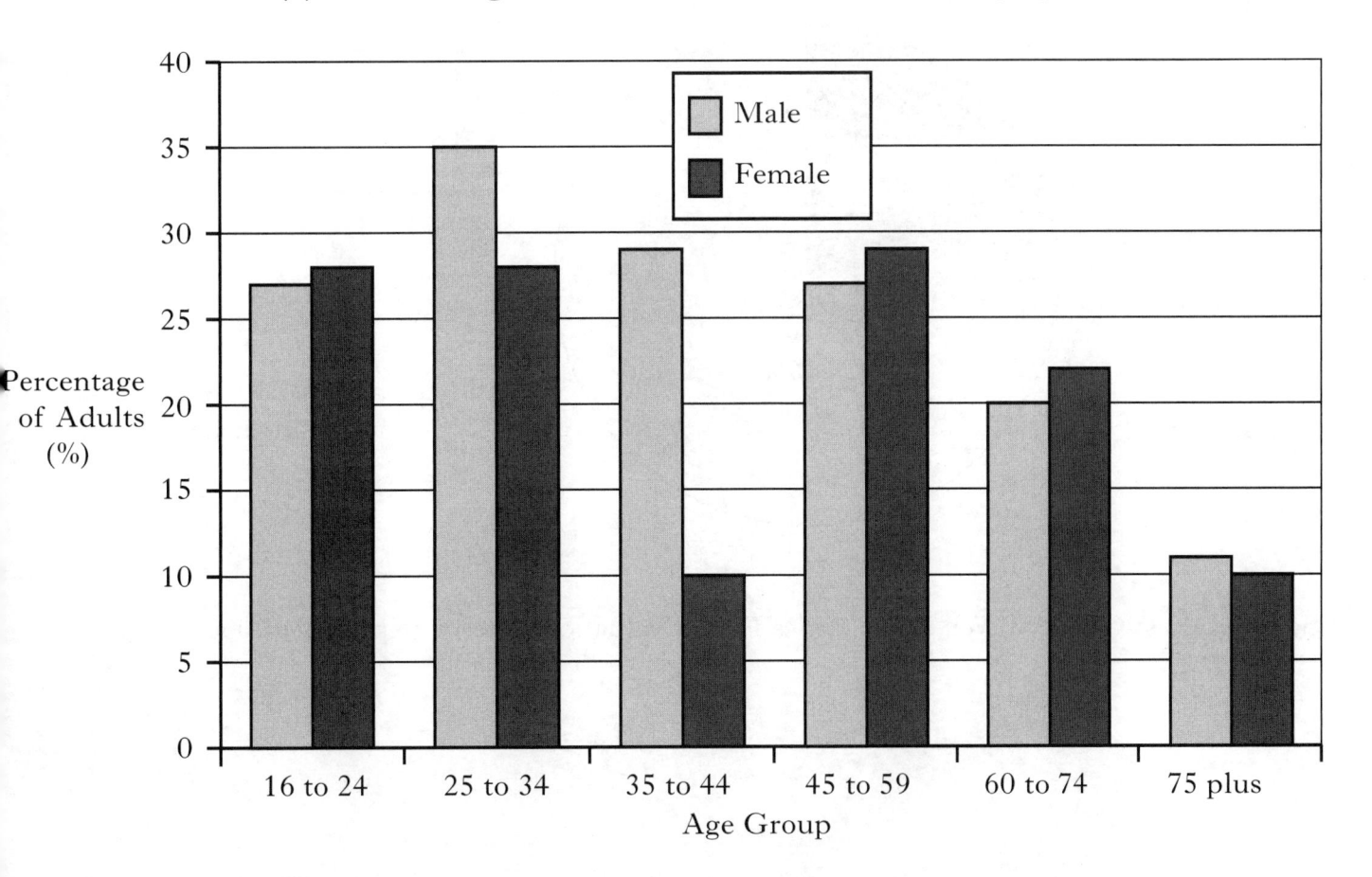

Both Sources: Adapted from Scottish Government data

SOURCE C: (continued)

SOURCE C3 SURVEY OF THE ATTITUDES OF MEN ATTENDING SOME OF THE WELL MAN CLINICS PILOT PROJECTS

SOURCE C3 (a) Were you happy with the information you received at the Well Man Clinics?

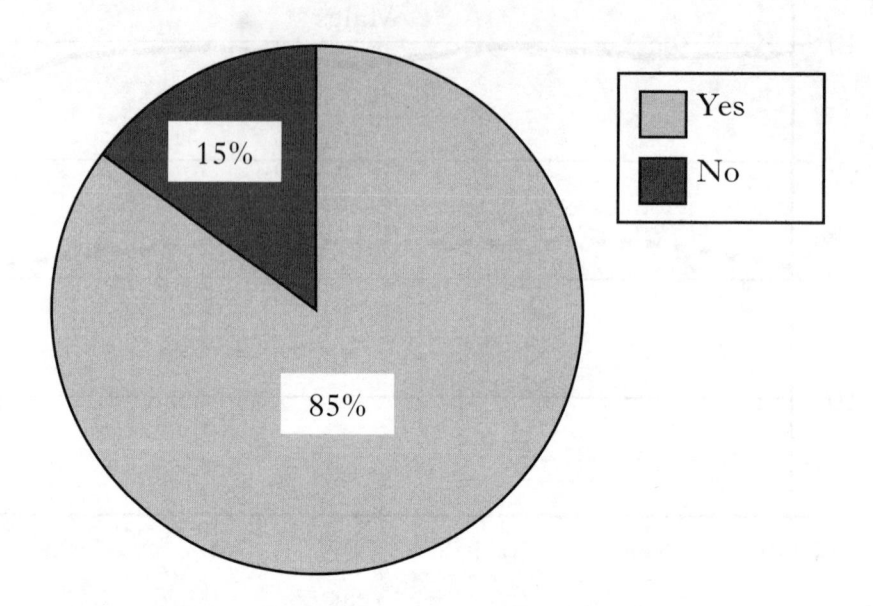

- Yes: 85%
- No: 15%

SOURCE C3 (b) Would you have liked to have seen Well Man Clinics open in the evenings?

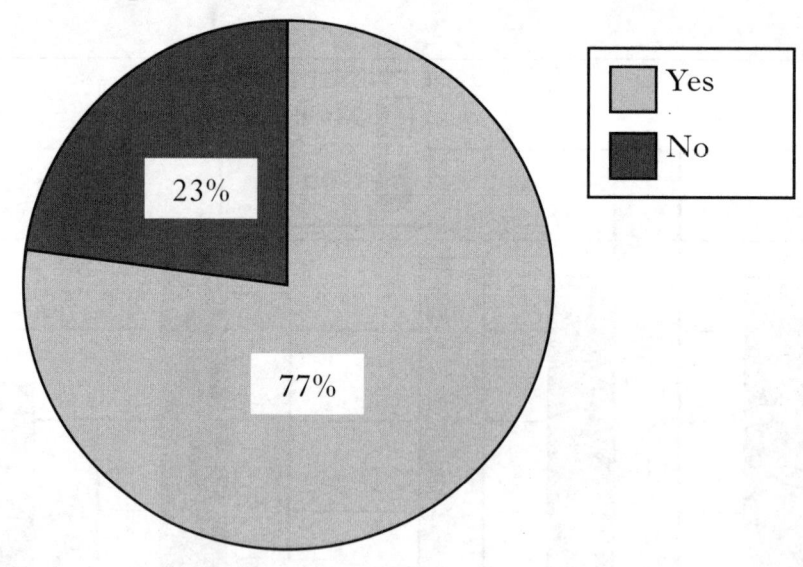

- Yes: 77%
- No: 23%

Source: East Glasgow Well Man Clinics Final Evaluation Report, September 2006

DECISION MAKING EXERCISE

Marks

QUESTIONS

Questions 1 to 3 are based on Sources A to C on Pages 2–6. Answer Questions 1 to 3 before attempting Question 4.

In Questions 1 to 3, use <u>only</u> the Sources described in each question.

Question 1

Use **only** *Source C1(a), Source C1(b) and Source A*.

To what extent does the evidence support Karen MacDonald? — **3**

Question 2

(*a*) Use **only** *Source C2(a) and Source A*.

Why might Karen MacDonald be accused of exaggeration? — **2**

(*b*) Use **only** *Source C2(b) and Source B*.

Why might William Walker be accused of exaggeration? — **2**

Question 3

Use **only** *Source C3(a), Source C3(b) and Source B*.

To what extent does the evidence support William Walker? — **3**

(10)

[X236/302]　　　　　　　　　*Page one* (*Insert*)

Question 4

Marks

> **DECISION MAKING TASK**
>
> You are a health policy adviser. You have been asked to prepare a report for the Scottish Government Cabinet Secretary for Health and Wellbeing in which you recommend or reject a proposal to introduce Well Man Clinics to every part of Scotland.
>
> Your answer should be written in the style of a *report*.
>
> Your report should:
>
> - recommend or reject the proposal to introduce Well Man Clinics to every part of Scotland
>
> - provide arguments to support your recommendation
>
> - identify and comment on any arguments which may be presented by those who oppose your recommendation
>
> - refer to all Sources provided
>   AND
>
> - **must** include relevant background knowledge.
>
> The written and statistical sources which are provided are:
>
> **SOURCE A:** Well Man Clinics are an Urgent Priority
>
> **SOURCE B:** Well Man Clinics are a Waste of Resources
>
> **SOURCE C:** Statistical Information

(20)

Total: 30 Marks

[*END OF QUESTION PAPER*]

HIGHER
2011

X236/301

NATIONAL
QUALIFICATIONS
2011

TUESDAY, 31 MAY
9.00 AM – 10.30 AM

MODERN STUDIES
HIGHER
Paper 1

Candidates should answer **FOUR** questions:

- **ONE** from Section A

and

- **ONE** from Section B

and

- **ONE** from Section C

and

ONE OTHER from **EITHER** Section A **OR** Section C

Section A: Political Issues in the United Kingdom
Section B: Social Issues in the United Kingdom
Section C: International Issues.

Each question is worth 15 marks.

SECTION A—Political Issues in the United Kingdom
Each question is worth 15 marks

STUDY THEME 1A: DEVOLVED DECISION MAKING IN SCOTLAND

Question A1

To what extent do Members of the Scottish Parliament (MSPs) influence decision making in the Scottish Government?

STUDY THEME 1B: DECISION MAKING IN CENTRAL GOVERNMENT

Question A2

Some groups outside Parliament have more influence on decision making in Central Government than others.

Discuss.

STUDY THEME 1C: POLITICAL PARTIES AND THEIR POLICIES (INCLUDING THE SCOTTISH DIMENSION)

Question A3

Political parties elect their leaders differently but the choice of leader is crucial to electoral success.

Discuss.

STUDY THEME 1D: ELECTORAL SYSTEMS, VOTING AND POLITICAL ATTITUDES

Question A4

Some factors affecting voting behaviour are more important than others.
Discuss.

SECTION B — Social Issues in the United Kingdom
Each question is worth 15 marks

STUDY THEME 2: WEALTH AND HEALTH INEQUALITIES IN THE UNITED KINGDOM

EITHER

Question B5

Poverty is the most important factor that affects health.

Discuss.

OR

Question B6

Health and welfare provision should be the responsibility of government.

Discuss.

[Turn over for Section C on *Page four*

SECTION C — International Issues
Each question is worth 15 marks

STUDY THEME 3A: THE REPUBLIC OF SOUTH AFRICA

Question C7

Assess the effectiveness of government policies to reduce social and economic inequalities in South Africa.

STUDY THEME 3B: THE PEOPLE'S REPUBLIC OF CHINA

Question C8

To what extent has social and economic change benefited the people of China?

STUDY THEME 3C: THE UNITED STATES OF AMERICA

Question C9

Assess the effectiveness of government policies to reduce social and economic inequalities in the USA.

STUDY THEME 3D: THE EUROPEAN UNION

Question C10

There is little disagreement within the EU over social and economic policies.

Discuss.

STUDY THEME 3E: THE POLITICS OF DEVELOPMENT IN AFRICA

Question C11

With reference to specific African countries (excluding the Republic of South Africa):

Education and health care are the most important factors in achieving successful development in Africa.

Discuss.

STUDY THEME 3F: GLOBAL SECURITY

Question C12

The UN must reform to be more effective when dealing with threats to international peace and security.

Discuss.

[END OF QUESTION PAPER]

X236/302

NATIONAL
QUALIFICATIONS
2011

TUESDAY, 31 MAY
10.50 AM – 12.05 PM

MODERN STUDIES
HIGHER
Paper 2

Summary of Decision Making Exercise

You are an independent policy researcher. You have been asked to prepare a report for the Low Pay Commission in which you recommend or reject a proposal to increase the value of the UK's National Minimum Wage (NMW) to £8 per hour for adult workers.

Before beginning the task, you must answer a number of evaluating questions (Questions 1–4) based on the source material provided. The source material is:

SOURCE A: A Living Wage of £8 per hour

SOURCE B: Unwelcome and Unaffordable

SOURCE C: Statistical Information

SOURCE A: A LIVING WAGE OF £8 PER HOUR

When introduced, the National Minimum Wage (NMW) was intended to end poverty wages for millions of low paid workers. Updated annually on the recommendation of the Low Pay Commission, the NMW sets a minimum hourly payment to which all workers are entitled. However, since 2007, the number of people on low incomes has risen while the relative value of the NMW in the UK is one of the lowest in the developed world. Therefore, if Government is serious in its attempts to meet its own targets to reduce poverty in this country, the NMW for adult workers should be increased to £8 per hour.

Lifting people out of poverty through work is widely seen as the best way to tackle inequality in society. Those who favour a collectivist approach understand the value of a more equal society. In recent years, the extent to which society has become more divided has become all too clear. There is a wealth of evidence that shows poverty, and the social problems poverty creates, is increasing. Tinkering with the tax and benefits system has not reduced the levels of poverty in this country. Radical change is required.

There will be many benefits arising from increasing the adult NMW to £8 per hour. To begin with, the embarrassing, complicated and costly process of means-tested benefits could be scrapped. An £8 per hour NMW is simple, straightforward, dignified and makes work pay. It would mean an end to employers paying poverty wages with the State making up the difference between low wages and what is needed to avoid hardship. Each low paid worker will immediately receive an increase in income. Jobs that were previously hard to fill because of low pay will become more attractive. In time, employers will benefit from a more stable, better rewarded and better committed workforce. Demand for goods will rise, leading to higher employment levels. In the years to come, Government will benefit through increased tax returns and reduced Social Security payments. Few people believe that an £8 per hour NMW will push up wage rates in other areas of employment. An £8 NMW is a "win-win" scenario.

To those who oppose £8 per hour NMW I say this: the UK cannot compete with the emerging nations of China, India and Brazil when it comes to low skilled manufacturing jobs. If our economy is to grow, the country must look to develop a highly skilled, highly rewarded workforce. The current NMW does not encourage unemployed people to move into paid employment. Many politicians believe that the NMW is too low. Introducing an £8 per hour NMW will energise our workforce and bring an end to poverty wages once and for all.

Ken Dorward, Anti-poverty Campaigner

SOURCE B: UNWELCOME AND UNAFFORDABLE

Demands to increase the adult National Minimum Wage (NMW) to £8 per hour must be resisted by the Low Pay Commission. At a time when the UK economy is only slowly recovering from the worst recession in fifty years, it would be economic madness to burden employers with extra wage costs. Every year since its introduction there has been a rise in the annual percentage rate of the NMW. In some years, the annual percentage rise in the NMW has been greater than the annual percentage rise in average earnings. The UK now has very few households living in poverty compared to other European Union countries. The rates of pay for the NMW currently ensure there are no poverty wages in this country. An £8 adult NMW is simply not needed.

There is a second reason why an £8 per hour adult NMW must be resisted. It is not the responsibility of government to reduce poverty—it is up to the individual to work harder, be better educated and become more skilled. Only when individuals strive to improve themselves can people be permanently lifted out of poverty. All too often people of working age in this country expect the State to provide for them. There is already a huge range of benefits to support the poorest groups in society. The UK's "dependency culture" must come to an end.

People work hard to ensure the success of their businesses. In the modern economy, wage levels reflect the value placed on different workers by society. Why should workers with the least skills and fewest qualifications be paid more than they are worth? Opinion surveys show that the public agree with the idea of an NMW but an £8 NMW would have a disastrous effect on businesses such as hotels and restaurants where the majority of low paid workers are found. In a world where multinational companies move from country to country seeking ever cheaper wage rates, our foreign competitors will hardly be able to believe their luck. In a number of countries in Europe, such as Denmark and Italy, there is no NMW and for good reason: it is unwelcome and unaffordable.

Supporters of an £8 adult NMW must consider the knock-on effect of their proposal. If wages for the lowest paid are increased, other workers will demand higher wages. Employers will be faced with rising wage demands that they simply cannot afford. To meet the cost of an £8 adult NMW employers will have to lay off staff at a time when UK unemployment rates are historically high. Trade union industrial action will be sure to follow. It is clear that those groups demanding an £8 adult NMW have not considered fully the consequences of their proposal.

Christine Kelly, Businessperson

[Turn over for Source C on *Pages four, five* and *six*

SOURCE C: STATISTICAL INFORMATION

SOURCE C1 Numbers of people in the UK on low incomes in millions 1979–2009

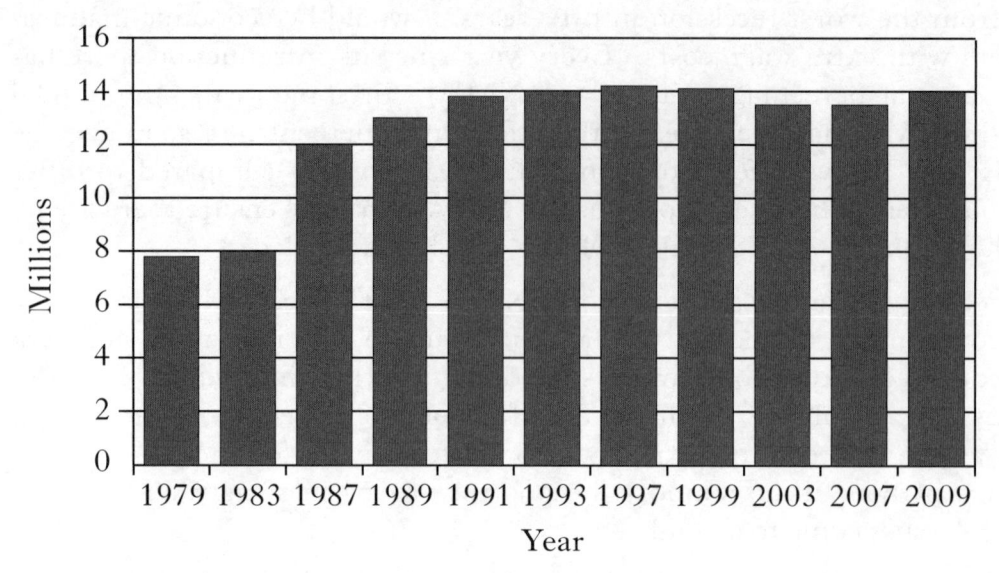

Source: Adapted from the Poverty Site

SOURCE C2 Comparison of the relative value of the national minimum wage in Pounds (£s) between selected developed countries, 2008

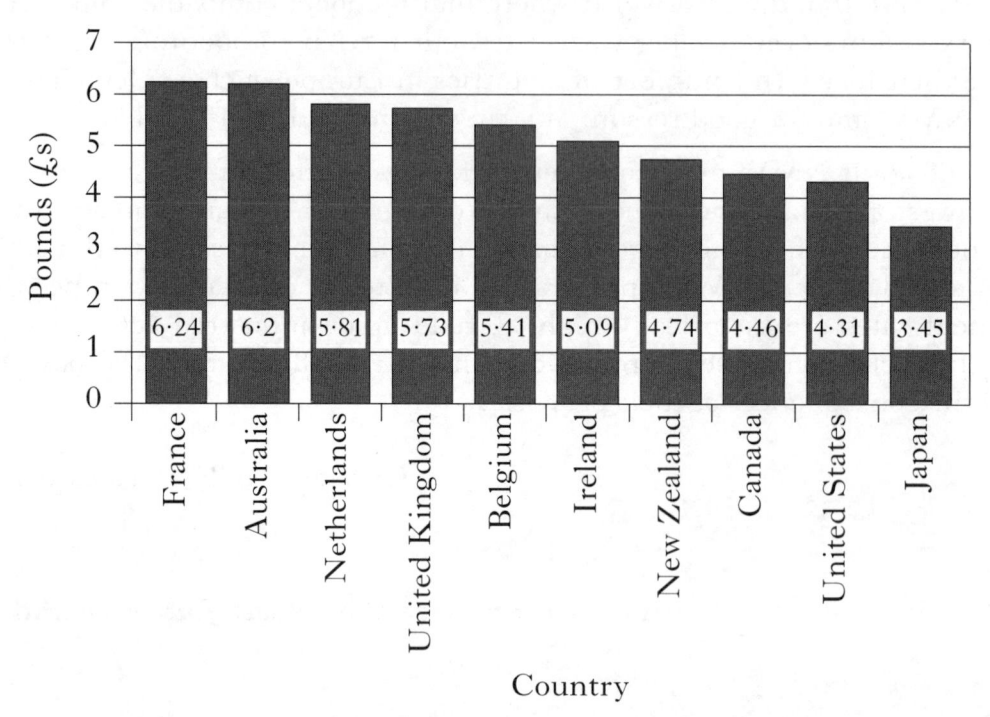

Country	Pounds (£s)
France	6·24
Australia	6·2
Netherlands	5·81
United Kingdom	5·73
Belgium	5·41
Ireland	5·09
New Zealand	4·74
Canada	4·46
United States	4·31
Japan	3·45

*The bar graph gives the value of the adult hourly NMW in selected countries if paid in UK Pounds (£s)

Source: Adapted from Low Pay Commission Report 2009

SOURCE C: (CONTINUED)

SOURCE C3 Public opinion survey on the National Minimum Wage 2009

(i) Do you agree with the idea of a National Minimum Wage (NMW)?
Yes 85%   No 10%   Don't know 5%

(ii) Do you think that the current NMW is . . .
Too high?   15%   Too low?   35%
About right?   40%   Don't know.   10%

(iii) Do you think a higher NMW would harm the UK economy?
Yes 50%   No 35%   Don't know 15%

(iv) Do you think a higher NMW will push up wages in other areas of employment?
Yes 40%   No 35%   Don't know 25%

Source: UK telephone survey, 1004 people, August 2009 (adapted)

SOURCE C4 Percentage (%) of households in poverty in selected EU countries 2009

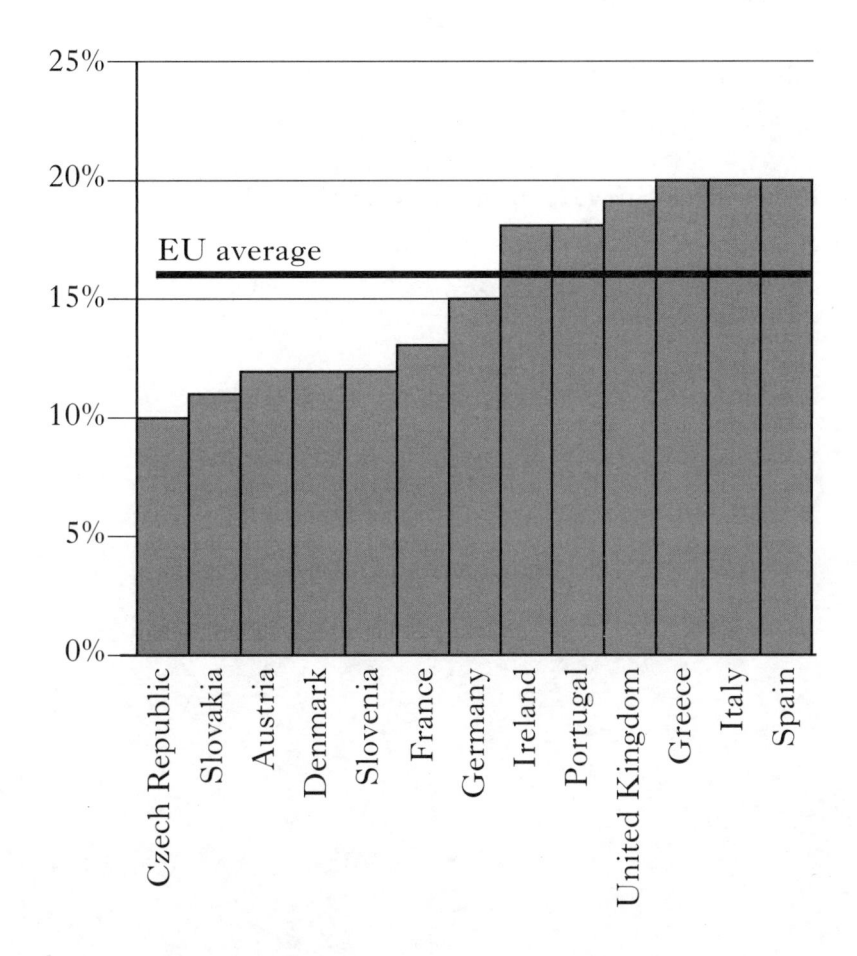

Country	%
Czech Republic	10%
Slovakia	11%
Austria	12%
Denmark	12%
Slovenia	12%
France	13%
Germany	15%
Ireland	18%
Portugal	18%
United Kingdom	19%
Greece	20%
Italy	20%
Spain	20%

EU average: 16%

Source: Adapted from Eurostat; updated Jan 2009

SOURCE C: (CONTINUED)

SOURCE C5 Types of employment where low paid workers were found [in percentages (%) in 2009]

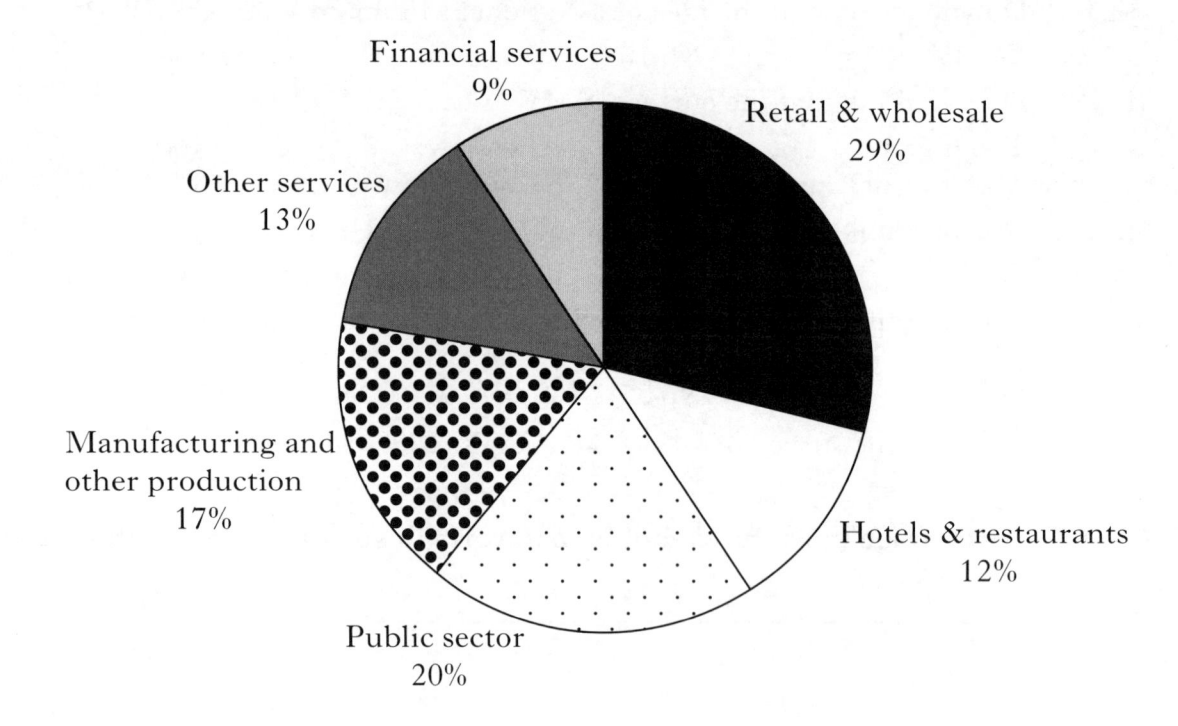

- Financial services 9%
- Retail & wholesale 29%
- Other services 13%
- Manufacturing and other production 17%
- Public sector 20%
- Hotels & restaurants 12%

Source: Adapted from Labour Force Survey; updated March 2009

DECISION MAKING EXERCISE

QUESTIONS

Marks

Questions 1 to 4 are based on Sources A to C on pages 2–6. Answer Questions 1 to 4 before attempting Question 5.

In Questions 1 to 4, use **only** the Sources described in each question.

Question 1

*Use **only** Source C1, C2 and Source A.*

To what extent does the evidence support Ken Dorward?   3

Question 2

*Use **only** Source C3 and Source A.*

Why might Ken Dorward be accused of exaggeration?   2

Question 3

*Use **only** Source C4 and Source B.*

Why might Christine Kelly be accused of exaggeration?   2

Question 4

*Use **only** Source C3, C5 and Source B.*

To what extent does the evidence support Christine Kelly?   3

    (10)

Question 5

Marks

DECISION MAKING TASK

You are an independent policy researcher. You have been asked to prepare a report for the Low Pay Commission in which you recommend or reject a proposal to increase the value of the UK's National Minimum Wage (NMW) to £8 per hour for adult workers.

Your answer should be written in the style of a *report*.

Your report should:

- recommend or reject the proposal to increase the UK's National Minimum Wage (NMW) to £8 per hour for adult workers
- provide arguments to support your recommendation
- identify and comment on any arguments which may be presented by those who oppose your recommendation
- refer to all the Sources provided

  AND

- **must** include relevant background knowledge.

The written and statistical sources which are provided are:

SOURCE A: A Living Wage of £8 per hour

SOURCE B: Unwelcome and Unaffordable

SOURCE C: Statistical Information

(20)

Total: 30 Marks

[END OF QUESTION PAPER]

Acknowledgements

Permission has been sought from all relevant copyright holders and Bright Red Publishing is grateful for the use of the following:

A table adapted from information from Labour Force Survey, Office for National Statistics © Crown Copyright. Reproduced under the terms of the Click-Use Licence (2007 Paper 2 page 4);

A graph adapted from Social Trends 2005 Edition No.35 © Crown Copyright. Reproduced under the terms of the Click-Use Licence (2007 Paper 2 page 5);

A chart and table adapted from information from The Department for Work and Pensions © Crown Copyright. Reproduced under the terms of the Click-Use Licence (2007 Paper 2 page 5);

Extracts adapted from Consultation on Review of NHS Prescription Charges (Scotland) 2007© Crown Copyright. Reproduced under the terms of the Click-Use Licence (2008 Paper 2 page 4);

A graph adapted from National Association of Citizens Advice Bureaux data 2001 (2008 Paper 2 page 4);

Extract adapted from SPICe Briefing, 2005 © Crown Copyright. Reproduced under the terms of the Click-Use Licence (2008 Paper 2 page 5);

Statistics © The Times/NI Syndication, June 2005 (2008 Paper 2 page 5).

Two tables 'Male and female death rates by selected causes in Scotland, 2003–2007' and 'Male and female life expectancy at birth in Scotland, 2005' © Crown copyright. Data supplied by General Register Office for Scotland. Reproduced under the terms of the Click-Use Licence (2010 Paper 2 page 4);

The graph 'Numbers of people in the UK on low incomes in millions 1979–2009' taken from The Poverty Site, www.poverty.org.uk © Guy Palmer (2011 Paper 2 page 4);

The graph 'Comparison of the relative value of the national minimum wage in Pounds (£s) between selected developed countries, 2008' adapted from the Low Pay Commission Report 2009 © Low Pay Commission (2011 Paper 2 page 4);

The graph 'Percentage (%) of households in poverty in selected EU countries 2009', adapted from Eurostat, © European Communities, 2009 (2011 Paper 2 page 5);

A graph adapted from Labour Force Survey, Office for National Statistics © Crown Copyright. Reproduced under the terms of the Click-Use Licence (2011 Paper 2 page 6).

HIGHER | ANSWER SECTION

BrightRED ANSWER SECTION FOR

SQA HIGHER
MODERN STUDIES 2007–2011

MODERN STUDIES HIGHER
PAPER 1
2007

Section A – Political Issues in the United Kingdom

Study Theme 1A – Devolved Decision Making in Scotland

Question A1

"Pass" and better answers should feature developed, exemplified knowledge and understanding of:
The reserved and devolved powers
Decisions arising from these made in Westminster and Holyrood respectively
and
Balanced comment on/analysis of the perceived 'importance' of these decisions for Scotland.

Answers may refer to:
- reserved powers include constitutional issues, defence, foreign policy, treasury matters and social security
- Westminster decides on the level of the Scottish Parliament's budget
- any revision of the Scotland Act must be passed by Westminster
- the 'Sewel Motion' procedure gives Westminster the power to legislate in an area supposedly devolved to Holyrood
- the range of devolved powers includes education, environment, health, justice and transport
- the Scottish Parliament has limited powers of taxation – it can vary (upwards or downwards) the rate of income tax by 3p in the £; it can vary the business rate – but has no fiscal autonomy
- laws passed by the Scottish Parliament include free personal care for the elderly; free nursery places for 3/4 year olds, free bus travel for pensioners, the abolition of tuition fees, a new voting system for local government, abolition of smoking in public places. *Candidates may comment on the importance of these (and others)*
- responsibility for agriculture and fisheries is devolved but the Scottish Parliament can only contribute as part of a UK delegation
- the Scottish Parliament cannot deal directly with Europe on issues such as crime, health and the environment, all of which are devolved
- the Home Office has rejected calls for tougher gun laws and limited the scope of the Fresh Talent Initiative
- despite a widely supported campaign north of the border, the Scottish Parliament could not prevent the amalgamation of the Scottish regiments
- Scotland not allowed a separate protocol on the forced removal of failed asylum seekers
- Westminster can decide how many nuclear power stations should be built but the Scottish Parliament decides on whether or not to award planning permission
- survey results have indicated that only 23% think that the Executive has most influence over how Scotland is run. A majority of voters see the reserved issues as the more important.
- in 2005, Jack McConnell wanted to review the responsibility for making laws on firearms restrictions, drugs, nuclear power stations, casinos, abortion, certain benefits, broadcasting and immigration – he was, reportedly, ordered to halt his "mission-creep" by Westminster
- in a YouGov poll (December 2006) 62% wanted the Scottish Parliament to have more powers
- other relevant points and issues.

Study Theme 1B – Decision Making in Central Government

Question A2

"Pass" and better answers should feature developed, exemplified knowledge and understanding of:
The powers of the Prime Minister
The opportunities afforded Parliament (Commons & Lords) to exercise control over these powers
and
Balanced comment on/analysis of the extent to which Parliament can control the powers of the Prime Minister.

Answers may refer to:
- powers of the Prime Minister derived from being party leader with the gift of patronage, leader of Her Majesty's Government, in charge of the Prime Minister's office, the leading UK representative on the world stage, the general election date decider, the Parliamentary link with the monarch.
- control traditionally seen as being exercised in both the Commons through debates, Prime Minister's Question Time, early day motions, select committees, inquiries, the Liaison Committee, the possibility of a no confidence motion, back bench revolts and in the House of Lords (in which at present, the Government does not have a majority)
- the Lib-Dems claim that the Salisbury Convention (do not oppose bills on which the winners campaigned) no longer stands
- claim that Parliament has seldom been more assertive than in recent years given the number of revolts in the Commons and the increase in the number of Government defeats in the Lords since the removal of most hereditary peers in 1999
- before 2001, Labour MPs accused of using Prime Minister's Question Time as a cringe-making competition in sycophancy. This changed in July 2001 when the Commons forced the Government to re-instate the chairs of each of the Foreign Affairs and Transport Select committees. In each vote over 100 Labour MPs voted against their own party
- over top-up fees, the Prevention of Terrorism Bill and the Religious Hatred Bill, the Government gave way on legislation in order to ensure its passage through the Commons
- Tony Blair did respond to the Butler Report's observation of his informal style of decision making by promising to curb his 'government by sofa'
- parliamentary control limited by the executive's control of the parliamentary timetable, the whip system, the payroll vote and the presidential nature of the Prime Minister's office
- Tony Blair's first ever defeat in the Commons was in November 2005 on the proposal to allow the detention of suspected terrorists for 90 days
- the rebellions over Iraq – the largest saw 139 Labour MPs defy the whip (2003) – were the largest on any policy since modern British party politics began
- two defeats during passage of the Racial and Religious Hatred Bill were as a result of a failure in whipping.
- the Prime Minister has better jobs to offer than the leader of the opposition, and has all the weight and expertise of the civil service to provide ministers with clever answers to awkward questions and can usually rely upon a healthy majority

- view that the only checks on the Prime Minister's power of patronage are informal – often through opinions voiced in the media (eg the coming to light in November 2005 of Tony Blair's proposals to award contributors to the political funds of the Labour and Conservative parties)
- parliament's role is to scrutinise not control
- other relevant points and issues.

Study Theme 1C – Political Parties and their Policies (including the Scottish Dimension)

Question A3

"Pass" and better answers should feature developed, exemplified knowledge and understanding of:

The importance of party unity to electoral success
Other factors that may enhance/damage electoral success
and
Balanced comment on/analysis of the importance of party unity in achieving electoral success.

Answers may refer to:

- with less electoral party loyalty than in the past, a united election campaign regarded as important to achieving electoral success
- damage was done to the Conservative Party by its obsession with Europe and its leadership wrangles
- electoral successes of 'new' (united) Labour
- link between 'quality' of leadership and perceived party unity, and its impact on polling indicators of electoral support
- impact of Cameron on support for the Conservative Party
- rivalries between 'old Labour' and the 'Blairites' and between Brown and Blair claimed to have been one explanation of Labour's poorer showing in 2005
- continued disagreement between 'fundamentalists' and 'gradualists' is said to have undermined electoral support for the SNP in the 2003 Scottish Parliament election in which SNP lost 8 MSPs, and its share of the vote fell to less than 20%
- disagreement evident in SNP leadership/ deputy leadership elections said to have damaged the party; 2005 General Election popular vote share was lowest since 1987, but did increase the number of MPs from 4 to 6 (the Salmond Bounce?)
- continued sniping at the quality of Charles Kennedy's leadership of the Liberal Democrats culminated in his resignation
- membership base (the Conservative Party membership has fallen from a peak of over 2 million to less than 250,000) and financial position. (Conservative Party reportedly clear of its £16m debt, January 2007, whilst Labour in debt to tune of £23m)
- the winning habit (importance of local elections)
- party policies on key issues
- the media and voters
- the electoral system (AMS) in Scotland
- view that parties have become more united in recent years as party policies have become less 'ideological' and differences between the main parties less ideological too
- other relevant points and issues.

Study Theme 1D – Electoral Systems, Voting and Political Attitudes

Question A4

"Pass" and better answers should feature developed, exemplified knowledge and understanding of:

The main voter "choice" and "representation" features of the AMS
The main voter "choice" and "representation" features of FPTP
and
Balanced comment on/analysis of whether the AMS or FPTP gives voters more choice and better representation.

Answers may refer to:

AMS
- voters have two votes: constituency and list
- there are no wasted votes
- degree of proportionality allows for wider range of parties featuring in the Scottish Parliament
- list can be used to increase minority representation and facilitate gender balance
- result likely to encourage consensus rather than conflict politics on the part of the elected, thus broadening voter representation at the highest decision-making level
- a greater proportion of voters likely to get a policy implemented that they voted for
- gives voters a range of representatives (8 in Scotland) from different parties to discuss an issue with

FPTP
- effective choice limited to marginal seats
- no proportionality
- wasted votes
- a large proportion of voters get neither an MP, nor the Government, nor the policy implementation that they voted for
- said to produce elected dictatorships; in 2005 Labour got 55% of the seats with 36% of the votes – the lowest winning party vote share in history
- in both systems the voter has little say in the selection of candidates
- in AMS closed party lists restricts voter choice as the parties need not name their candidates
- AMS still retains the so-called negative features of the constituency vote and is not wholly proportional, but more so than FPTP; in 2003 Labour polled 32% of the vote for its 38% seats
- There are no by-elections in AMS so voters denied 'protest-vote' opportunities or any say in who their new government representative should be
- AMS produces coalitions and compromise policies that no one voted for
- AMS produces disproportional representation in the Executive; the Liberal Democrats were the fourth most popular party with 13% of the vote (in 2003)
- the proportion of minority ethnic MPs is higher under FPTP in the House of Commons
- 33·3% of the Scottish Parliament is female; for Westminster the figure is 18%
- 'backdoor entry' to Parliament via the list may result in MSPs and even members of the Executive, for whom no one voted
- the role of the regional/list members is obscure. To whom are they accountable?
- arguably little evidence of consensus
- issues arising from the 2007 Scottish Parliamentary Election
- other relevant points and issues.

Section B – Social Issues in the United Kingdom

Study Theme 2 – Wealth and Health Inequalities in the United Kingdom

Question B5

"Pass" and better answers should feature developed, exemplified knowledge and understanding of:

The founding principles of the Welfare State
Government Welfare State/State welfare policies
and
Balanced comment on/analysis of the extent to which Government policies enable the founding principles of the Welfare State to be met.

Answers may refer to:
- solution to the problems of want, disease, ignorance, squalor and idleness seen in the 'traditional' collectivist approach
- benefits to provide social security to protect the population from cradle to the grave.

Income
- range of Government benefits available for those out of work, including Income Support and Jobseekers Allowance, becoming increasingly means tested
- the National Minimum Wage
- issue of paying for pensions
- launch of campaign against child poverty in 1999, child poverty in Scotland reduced by 25% (target) in 2005 (for UK by 23%)

Health
- evidence of inequalities between social classes and gender/race
- New Labour's "holistic" approach to health care; good-health promotion campaigns, bans on smoking; PPP; welfare to work strategies aim to improve the quality of life
- SureStart
- Government still provides care but asks individuals to take responsibility too
- issue of charges.

Education
- recent public and privately channelled investment in education
- issue of fees/loans for higher education
- Sure Start

Housing
- lack of available council housing
- impact of boom in property prices on first-time buyers
- role of housing associations
- housing benefit

Employment
- the welfare-to-work (a hand up, not a hand out) strategy
- Tax Credits
- New Deals
- Pathways to Work
- SureStart

- the idea of universalism has faced substantial pressure in the past few years
- instead of universal benefits that are largely flat rate, the expansion of means-testing, ('targeting') has led to the creation of benefits like Pension Credit and also tax credits
- Tax Credits are near universal benefits directed at all but the richest 10% of families with children
- progressive universalism
- proposals for incapacity benefit
- contributory principle under threat
- the idea of a state monopoly has been tempered to some degree by greater involvement of the private and voluntary sectors
- UK has one of the highest child poverty rates in developed countries
- labour market polarised between work-rich and work-poor households
- financial support for working parents is now amongst the most generous for low-paid employees in the OECD
- no set targets for reducing poverty in the population as a whole; work may reduce the risk of poverty but it does not eliminate it
- Government policy has been most successful in dealing with 'blockbuster' poverty – the poverty suffered by the greatest number of people – by giving the poor more money
- Government would insist that changes are in keeping with the concept of 'modern' collectivism
- other relevant points and issues.

Question B6
"Pass" and better answers should feature developed, exemplified knowledge and understanding of:
Inequalities in the UK
Government policies to reduce these inequalities and/or reasons for these inequalities
and
Balanced comment on/analysis of the extent to which inequalities continue to exist in the UK.

Answers may refer to:
Social and Economic Inequalities linked to age, gender, race, social class, region;
- huge inequalities in the way that care and support are made available to older people
- continued evidence of 'glass ceiling' (might be cracked, not yet broken). New 'glass partition' – women concentrated in the less well-paid sectors of the professions
- women still earning less than men in part-time and full-time jobs; men in full-time employment now earning 18% more an hour than women
- extent of racism
- ethnic minorities find it difficult to get jobs; and many are more likely to be unemployed than white males of the same age and level of education
- the social class wealth and health gap
- claim that the 'disadvantaged dying' become part of the 'revolving door' system; labelled as 'bed blockers' as if being ill and not getting treatment were their own fault
- North-South wealth and health divide
- gap in living standards between the well paid and those on benefits
- lone-parent families
- continued existence of poverty: view that the UK's most troubled group, in both absolute and relative terms, is poor, white and British born
- expansion of the middle class has made it harder than ever for the working classes to get better high-earning professional jobs
- all groups have become more prosperous but the gap between the classes has not narrowed
- North-South split widening; difference within regions; Glasgow labelled 'a swamp of poverty' because all ten of the most deprived areas in Scotland are in the city (Scottish Index of Multiple Deprivation); Northern areas of England have higher obesity rates, more smoking related deaths and lower life expectancies than Southern areas
- view that gender equality is no longer a live issue – girls are high achievers at school; high % of MSPs are women; Solicitor General is a woman; opening up of medicine, the legal profession and the church (where there is an increasing demand for part-time clergy) to women
- General Household Survey analysis shows that UK born ethnic minorities seem to be doing the same jobs as similarly qualified whites and earning similar amounts
- children of Afro-Caribbean and Indian immigrants have closed the earnings gap with whites in both professional and blue-collar work
- other relevant points and issues

Government/local policies/strategies to reduce inequalities:
- promise to end child poverty forever
- gender and race legislation
- Equalities Act (2006) - under the Act the Commission for Equality and Human Rights (CEHR) will bring together the Disability Rights Commission and the Equal Opportunities Commission from October 2007. The Commission for Racial Equality will join in 2009, putting expertise on equality, diversity and human rights all in one place
- other relevant points and issues.

Section C – International Issues

Study Theme 3A – The Republic of South Africa

Question C7

"Pass" and better answers should feature developed, exemplified knowledge and understanding of:
The *democratic* features of the South African political system
The part played by the ANC and other political groups in the South African political system
and
Balanced comment on/analysis of the suggestion that South Africa has become a one party state.

Answers may refer to:
- South Africa is a constitutional democracy with a three tier system of government and an independent judiciary
- Party List Electoral system
- 16 parties represented in parliament
- 97 parties contested the 2006 elections
- President, elected by the National Assembly, is permitted to serve a maximum of two five-year terms (but nothing, technically, to prevent someone serving a third term as president of the ANC)
- written Constitution and Constitutional Court
- Constitutional (Bill of Rights) guarantees include property rights and education
- free press and a robust legal system
- recognition of trade unionism
- ANC has a huge majority in the National Assembly and is the dominant party in the provinces
- there are 6 non-black 'co-opted' cabinet members
- ANC has not tampered with the Constitution and accepted decisions of the Constitutional court
- no concept of a 'loyal opposition'; the Democratic Alliance Party, the second largest in the National Assembly has 50 seats (ANC has 285) out of 400
- ANC is said to dismiss ideas from outside its own bureaucracy (eg response to the HIV/AIDS crisis) and to meet any criticism with accusations of racism
- claims by Desmond Tutu of the emergence of a culture of 'sycophantic obsequious conformity'
- some SABC commentators blacklisted in 2006 for being too critical of the Government; judges and journalists are told to 'work together to build the nation'
- Inkatha Freedom Party claims that the ANC is determined to alter or remove the legislative authority of the provinces and warns against the danger of South Africa becoming a one party state
- COSATU plays little part in economic policy decisions
- Jacob Zuma on record as claiming that the ANC will remain in office 'until Jesus comes back'
- ANC remains extremely popular; its vote share has risen in each of three elections (1994/1999/2004) due to a combination of factors: the struggle to end apartheid and bring democracy/its record in office/the opposition parties are so weak
- other relevant points and issues.

Study Theme 3B – The People's Republic of China

Question C8

"Pass" and better answers should feature developed, exemplified knowledge and understanding of:
Recent social and economic reform policies of the Chinese Government
The impact of these reforms on Chinese society
and
Balanced comment on/analysis of the overall effects of social and economic reform.

Answers may refer to:
- relaxation of the hukuo – urban/rural classification of population
- dismantling of the danwei – work unit behaviour control organisation
- relaxation in rural areas of One Child Policy
- reduction in waiting time for those who qualify to have a second child
- better rights for women
- development of private education and health services
- right to own property now written into the Constitution
- encouragement of foreign investment
- promotion of capitalist ideas – introduction of easier credit for business, support for entrepreneurs
- increase in subsidies and greater investment in agriculture
- tax reform
- 'great development of the west' policy to boost development in western regions
- awarding of the 'dragonhead status' to favoured districts
- gradual changes to the judicial system: increased legal representation
- huge and sustained rises in economic growth
- incomes have risen in the cities, particularly in the coastal areas
- mining held up as an example of the success of policy to invest in the west of China
- claim that the number of poor has fallen sharply in recent years
- greater social freedoms
- expanding wealthy middle class and greatly improved standard of living
- paper recycling tycoon Zhang Yin became the first woman to top China's rich list in October 2006
- uneven rise in farm income
- as a result of tax reform and subsidies, rural incomes have increased but urban incomes have grown much faster
- huge urban/rural and employed/unemployed income/lifestyle inequalities
- homelessness and overcrowding in the large cities exacerbated by migration
- poor working conditions in many factories
- allegations of corruption on the part of local CPC officials in managing change
- the UN Development Programme claims that 50 million farmers have been thrown off the land with little or no compensation
- 20-30 million State Owned Enterprise workers have lost their jobs
- widespread and sustained rural protest: 87,000 'contradictions within the people' recorded in 2005
- problems associated with pollution
- other relevant points and issues.

Study Theme 3C – The United States of America

Question C9

"Pass" and better answers should feature developed, exemplified knowledge and understanding of:
Ethnic minority participation in elections in the USA
The importance of the minority ethnic vote/ethnic minority issues to the outcome of elections in the USA
and
Balanced comment on/analysis of the extent to which ethnic minorities influence the outcome of elections in the USA.

Answers may refer to:
- minorities make up 30% of the US population and their population share is growing, with Hispanics being the fastest growing

- minority groups less likely to either register or vote than Whites; only African Americans have registration and turnout in excess of 50%
- registration of APIs and Hispanics is less than 40% and turnout fails to reach 30%
- for Whites registration is almost 68% and turnout just above 60%
- concentration on ethnic minority voters in key 'swing states' of California, Texas, New York and Florida gives them disproportionate influence in the presidential elections
- growing potential impact of the Hispanic vote in Arizona, Colorado, Nevada and New Mexico
- traditionally the ethnic minority vote has gone to the Democratic Party; although a majority for Kerry in 2004, Bush still won the presidential elections
- importance of the ethnic minority vote recognised in the composition of the Bush Cabinet
- Blacks are most solid in their support of the Democrats (90%); for Hispanics the level of support is 55% and for APIs, 59%
- Democrats use a variety of methods to get out the minority vote. Republicans more likely to be accused of using "dirty tricks" to prevent black voters getting to the polls
- most of the Black Democrats in Congress come from majority Black districts
- at local levels, electoral success may depend upon involvement of ethnic minority voters in a coalition with Whites; Antonio R Villariagosa, LA's first Latino mayor since 1872 was elected in 2005, with 59% of the vote by forging a coalition that included Black voters as well as Latinos and Whites
- nine Indian Americans were winners in the November 2006 US elections to national, state and local offices including Minnesota State Senator Chaudhary (Democrat) whose constituency is largely White
- view that Hispanic voters, annoyed by the Republican hard line on immigration, turned out in force, and helped the Democrats win the November 2006 congressional elections
- both Hillary Clinton and Barrack Obama courting the minority vote in their presidential candidate campaigns
- thanks to gerrymandering and the ease with which those in power can raise money, usually 90% of those who run for the House of Representatives tend to be re-elected
- importance of **gender** (women have tended to be more significantly supportive of the Democrat candidate than men); **religion** (Protestants more pro-Republican and Catholics more pro-Democrat) and the 'religious right'; the '**wealth gap**' – not as influential as it was; **geographic region**, with the Northeast having become the new heartland of the Democratic Party and the Republicans now in control of the socially conservative South
- in congressional (and presidential) elections the big issues are at present terrorism, the war in Iraq, the economy and jobs and moral issues. However, an alleged racial slur said to have cost the incumbent George Allen (Virginia) his seat in the Senate, losing to the Democrat James Webb by 0.3% of the vote
- other relevant points and issues.

Study Theme 3D – The European Union

Question C10

"Pass" and better answers should feature developed, exemplified knowledge and understanding of:
The main agreed social and economic policies of the EU
Issues on which there is disagreement amongst the current membership
and
Balanced comment on/analysis of the extent to which there is agreement on social and economic policies in the EU.

Answers may refer to:
Agreed aims of:
- regional policy
- social policies
- common agricultural policy
- fisheries policy
- economic policy.

Disagreement 'issues':
- criteria for regional aid
- the working time directive
- response to UK proposal on a prison transfer scheme
- reform of CAP and the UK rebate issue
- response to the ETS (emissions trading scheme)
- fish stock protection measures and quotas: allegations that some national enforcement agencies are less efficient than others; resistance to reform by entrenched interests in Spain, France, Portugal and Greece
- single currency; 13 countries 'in' and 3 'out'
- single market; consequences of economic migration
- the budget
- further enlargement
- an EU constitution
- foreign policy
- rules for accepting workers from Eastern Europe
- other relevant points and issues.

Study Theme 3E – The Politics of Development in Africa

Question C11

"Pass" and better answers should feature developed, exemplified, knowledge and understanding with reference to specific African countries (excluding the Repulic of South Africa) of:
The contribution of sources/forms of foreign aid to the development needs of African countries
Factors that may limit the impact of foreign aid on development
and
Balanced comment on/analysis of the suggestion that foreign aid alone is no guarantee of development.

Answers may refer to:
- sources of foreign aid: international; governmental; non-governmental; the forms they take (grants, donations, loans, advice, short- and long-term projects, food aid etc) and their contribution to development
- the Millennium Development Goals: eradication of extreme poverty and hunger; achievement of universal primary education; promotion of gender equality and empowerment of women; reduction in child mortality; improvement in maternal health; combating HIV/AIDS, malaria and other diseases; environmental sustainability; global partnership for development
- misuse of aid – not only confined to military spending by those in authority. In Nigeria, bed nets for protection against the mosquito were made into wedding gowns
- money does not always go where it is intended
- consequences of civil and international strife
- questions over the relevance of some aid: many threats to public health do not need hospitals, highly trained clinicians or expensive medical treatment. On the other hand there is no good in handing out AIDS drugs without the infrastructure to back them up through major investment in nurses, hospitals, sanitation and utilities
- terms of trade policies of the developed world
- view that DOHA did not deliver because of the trade policies of poor countries. 50% of what developing countries would gain from fully free trade would come from their own tariff cuts because 1/3 of their exports are to other poor countries and their tariffs are much higher (many relying on tariffs as a source of revenue)

- view that trade liberalisation is no substitution for either domestic reform or foreign aid
- view that if Africa increased its share of world trade by just 1%, it would bring an extra £34b per annum (five times what it receives in aid). Freer trade would cut the number of Sub-Saharan Africans in absolute poverty by 60 million
- "aid without trade is a lullaby – a song you sing to children to get them to sleep" (Yoweri Musevini)
- selective approach of Heavily Indebted Poor Countries Initiative – debts of Somalia and Sudan have not been dropped
- view that wiping out debt acts as a disincentive to those trying to become financially stable and rewards those that do not
- problems of so-called 'failed states' whose people suffer from 'bad governance'
- NEPAD has accepted that in order to secure foreign aid, African governments must reform and be more transparent in their use of aid from Developed Nations
- claims that aid causes corruption, creates dependency and discourages entrepreneurship
- view that addressing infrastructure impediments is the most effective way to stimulate poverty reduction and economic growth
- even when aid is 'properly' used, development does not come overnight; when Zambia's foreign debt was reduced, most of the savings spent on recruiting teachers and improving health care (fees for basic health care removed). Nevertheless, Zambia remains poor and still depends on aid
- recognition by both the UN Investing in Development: A Practical Plan to achieve the Millennium Goals and the Commission for Africa that "more aid is needed to meet Africa's development needs". However "outsiders cannot deliver development, it must be done by Africans" (Commission for Africa report)
- Millennium Project has set up 12 'research villages' (target of 1000 by 2009) in 10 African countries to pioneer models of development (The Magnificent Seven) that can be copied but there is an admission that successful implementation depends upon foreign aid
- other relevant points and issues

Study Theme 3F – Global Security

Question C12

"Pass" and better answers should feature developed, exemplified knowledge and understanding of:
Threats to global security
Sources (candidates may select from UN, NATO, AU, EU, USA and coalition allies) and forms of international responses to threats to global security
and
Balanced comment on/analysis of the effectiveness of international responses to threats to global security.

Answers may refer to:

Threats:
- civil conflict
- international disputes
- nuclear proliferation
- post-conflict recovery (peace building)
- terrorism
- unstable regimes

Responses:
- UN – Democratic Republic of the Congo, Eritrea, Lebanon, Ethiopia, Sudan; response to acquisition of nuclear weapons by North Korea
- NATO – Bosnia, Macedonia, Kosovo, Afghanistan (where in October 2006 it took charge of Afghanistan's eastern provinces, which had been under the control of US forces since Taliban ousted in 2001)
- African Union – Sudan (forces airlifted there by EU and NATO)
- EU – Bosnia, where EUFOR took over control of peacekeeping operations from NATO in February 2005 (80% of the force simply changed badges); diplomatic response to Iran's nuclear ambitions
- USA (and coalition allies) – Iraq and The War on Terrorism against 'the axis of evil'
- 2005 Rand Corporation study of American and UN peacekeeping operations concluded that UN missions were not only cheaper, but had higher success rate and enjoyed greater international legitimacy
- Canadian study attributed the dramatic decline in the number of conflicts in the past decade to the "huge increase" in preventative diplomacy and peacekeeping "for the most part authorised and mounted by the UN"
- for most of the UN's history the powerful have by-passed the Security Council when they chose to
- UN is hampered by its Charter, veto, and modus operandi: fact finding mission > Security Council approval > need to find peacekeepers
- UN resolutions ignored by members
- sanction breaking
- AU initially turned down offer of UN help in Darfur
- initial refusal of Sudanese government to allow UN intervention in Darfur, accusing the UN of being an agent of the West. However, it agreed to allow in a 'hybrid' UN and AU force
- Sudan has the backing of China and Russia who consistently water-down attempts to impose sanctions
- UN resolution 1718 (October 2006) belatedly imposed sanctions on North Korea (China had hitherto blocked) but included no reference to military intervention as USA had proposed
- USA lobby to put an American in charge of all UN peacekeeping operations seen as a move that could offer Washington an exit strategy in Iraq. (USA contributes 0.5% of UN peacekeepers)
- despite its headline failures, the scandalous behaviour of some corrupt officials and the unacceptable behaviour of some of its peacekeepers, the UN is still regarded as an essential organisation for achieving a better, fairer, more peaceful world
- view that the UN Secretary General (Ban Ki-moon) cannot succeed without Washington's co-operation and reform of the organisation
- election held in the DR (Democratic Republic) Congo (2006)
- EU unable to agree over either war in Iraq (2001-2003) or Israel's war in Lebanon
- difficulties facing NATO in defeating the Taliban militarily
- USA-British difficulties in Iraq
- other relevant points and issues.

MODERN STUDIES HIGHER
PAPER 2
DECISION MAKING EXERCISE
2007

1. Russell Barclay claims (Source A) that "long-term sickness and disability is the most common reason given by both men and women for not working".
   Source C1 shows this to be true of men but not of women.

2. (a) Russell Barclay claims (Source A) that "the UK already spends a greater percentage of its GDP on schemes for disabled workers than any other country in the EU".
   Source C2(a) shows that the UK spends less than most of the other EU countries listed.
   (b) Irene Graham claims (Source B) that charities already "spend more on the disabled than on any other group".
   Source C2(b) shows that more is spent on children.

3. Irene Graham claims (Source B) that "UK Government spending on the sick and disabled is already lower than for any other group and a lower percentage of one-parent families receive Incapacity/Disability Benefit than any other benefit".
   Source C3(a) shows spending on (any one of) three other groups to be lower.
   Source C3(b) shows that, for the benefits listed, 9% (by far the lowest) of one-parent families receive Incapacity/Disability Benefit.

4. **Credit:**
   A style appropriate to a report (sub-headings, chapters etc) with:
   - an introduction that indicates an awareness of the role to be adopted and makes a clear recommendation
   - developed arguments in support of the recommendation
   - identification of and comment on (rebuttal of) counter arguments
   - synthesis of source information
   - provision and use of appropriate background knowledge
   - an overall conclusion.

Arguments for the proposal may feature:
- increased spending must be brought under control
- evidence that not all claimants are incapable of work
- proposal maintains original aims of the welfare state in encouraging work/discouraging idleness
- work is now less physically demanding
- work is beneficial to the individual
- provision of useful training for those who can work
- genuine claimants will be better off
- existing recipients of IB not affected.

Arguments against the proposal may feature:
- reduction in number of claimants already happening as the existing system is already a tough one
- charities have to underpin an under-funded welfare state
- increased stress on vulnerable individuals
- concern of experts over implications
- priority should be to overcome employer prejudice
- UK spends less on helping disabled workers than most EU states
- original aims of the welfare state being compromised
- yet another money saving device.

Credit background knowledge-based argument, developed from references in:
Source A
- *We are encouraging welfare dependency at the expense of individual responsibility.*
- *…and give the taxpayer better value for their money.*
- *We are determined to continue to move people from welfare into work.*
- *…the fundamental principles of the welfare state.*

Source B
- *…the cost of the welfare state.*
- *…other groups vulnerable to poverty, such as lone-parents.*
- *"Welfare to Work" policies.*
- *Effective laws to prevent discrimination against the disabled.*
- *…social exclusion and…the collectivist principles of the welfare state.*

Other background knowledge-based arguments may include:
- the long-term increase in the cost of social welfare which was not anticipated by Beveridge (infinite demand for finite resources)
- whether or not the proposal is in conflict with the original aims of the welfare state
- the extent and causes of poverty in the UK
- political debate: Labour back-bench revolt over IB reform; policy differences between Blairites and traditional Labour
- foreign comparisons
- recent media coverage
- other relevant issues/points.

MODERN STUDIES HIGHER
PAPER 1
2008

Section A – Political Issues in the United Kingdom

Study Theme 1A: Devolved Decision Making in Scotland

Question A1

"Pass" and better answers should feature developed, exemplified knowledge and understanding of:

The part played by local government (responsibilities and decision making powers) in a devolved Scotland

The limitations on local government decision making powers and responsibilities in a devolved Scotland

and

Balanced comment on/analysis of the role of local government in decision making in a devolved Scotland.

Answers may refer to:

- local government serves, represents and is accountable to, the people of different communities.
- delivery of cost-effective local services (mandatory, permissive, discretionary): importance of these.
- *Public Attitudes to Local Government in Scotland* report highlighted that throughout the UK the institution of local government is not well thought of. Generally perceived to be bureaucratic, inefficient and wasteful of public money.
- services more highly regarded than the institution.
- 38% (2005 Scottish Household Survey) agreed that their council was addressing the key issues affecting the quality of life in their neighbourhood.
- one of the principles of local government is 'inclusion for all', hence, recent injection of cash into modernising facilities and getting young people involved in physical activity.
- setting and collection of the Council Tax; 'concordat' between SNP led administration and COSLA to freeze council tax until 2010; less ring fencing of grants; councils may retain any efficiency savings they make.
- Scottish Government works in partnership with local authorities in making decisions and delivering services.
- local government issues can now be fully aired and debated in the Scottish Parliament and its committees.
- councils have better access to ministers and civil servants than previously.
- three year funding has given councils the chance to plan ahead and have brought greater financial stability.
- changes to Scottish Enterprise involve the transfer of 'local' responsibilities to local authorities. The responsibility for providing local business support to be handed to local councils. Move recognises the role of local authorities as players in economic development.
- Scottish Government is the top tier of government vested with the powers to legislate on local government and on Scottish domestic functions.
- majority of local government income derived from Rate Support Grant and other Scottish Government monies; weighting of grants dependent on need/ability of councils to raise Council Tax/non domestic rates.
- councils increasingly forced to implement policies they do not support, for example, PFI/PPP, 'Best Value'; concerns over funding of Free Personal Care.
- reduction in council role: social housing provided through housing stock transfers.
- council planning decisions can be, and are, overturned by the Scottish Government; Donald Trump Golf Resort issue has raised questions about the role of local government in big development projects and effectiveness of planning procedures.
- claim that local government's share of public spending has fallen to an all-time low, whilst that of unelected and unaccountable 'quangos' has risen; this seen as an affront to local democracy.
- claim that devolution has undermined the status of local government. Pre-devolution, local government got greater media coverage. Full-time, all Scotland local government correspondents no longer exist as press attention and resources now focused on Parliament.
- implications of SNP's first budget 2007. Promised not to cut the number of councils. Withdrew previous threats of penalties for overspending. Extra funding - not ring-fenced. Seen as giving COSLA greater flexibility and responsibility.
- other relevant points.

Study Theme 1B: Decision Making in Central Government

Question A2

"Pass" and better answers should feature developed, exemplified knowledge and understanding of:

- The ways in which pressure groups attempt to influence decision making in Central Government
- The impact (successes/failures) of pressure groups on decision making in Central Government

and

- Balanced comment on/analysis of the effectiveness of pressure groups in influencing decision making in Central Government.

Answers may refer to:

- campaigns, protests, demonstrations, use of media, lobbying, petitions, e-petitions, letter writing, direct action, sponsorship of political candidates, etc.
- sectional/interest groups and promotional/cause groups.
- insider/outsider groups.
- both the number and range of pressure groups have increased in recent years; growth of single-issue groups.
- under Labour the number of sources of political power has increased and there are more decision-makers for groups to try to influence; the implementation of devolution has created new power hubs for pressure groups to focus on.
- importance of access to Government and compatibility with Government thinking; size and type of membership, funds, and tactics; prevailing social/economic/political climate; level of public support.
- a pressure group might be part of the relevant policy community on some issues but excluded on others; in the Foot and Mouth epidemic of 2001, the NFU prevented an inoculation programme but the earlier fuel protests were in part created by the fact that many smaller farmers felt they were being ignored by the government.
- despite student protest marches against proposed top-up fees, the government went ahead with proposals.
- refusal of government to introduce PR for Parliamentary elections signified the limited influence of Charter 88.
- CBI seen as clear winners; CND as clear losers. In recent years there have been more 'smaller' winners; fewer 'larger' winners.
- successful 2005 Jamie Oliver initiative to persuade the government to allocate bigger subsidies to school meals.
- failure of the Stop the War (mobilised greater numbers on the streets than Make Poverty History) and the Countryside Alliance campaigns.
- Make Poverty History campaign seen (in hindsight) as a qualified success.

- declining influence of traditional campaigning has led to pressure groups contesting elections.
- success not always measured simply in policy outcome terms, rather the extent of engagement of the political establishment.
- so far, although there are lots of e-petitions on Number 10's website, they have mostly just allowed the disgruntled to let off steam.
- other relevant points.

Study Theme 1C: Political Parties and their Policies (Including the Scottish Dimension)

Question A3

"Pass" and better answers should feature developed, exemplified knowledge and understanding of:
- Political party policies selected from the following: law and order; taxation; education; Europe
- Differences and similarities between these policies

and
- Balanced comment on/analysis of the assertion that there are few policy differences between the main political parties.

Answers may refer to:
- *Law and Order*
  (Westminster 2005)
    - **Labour**: dedicated policing teams for every area; 25,000 community support officers; 1,300 more prison places; double the cash for drug treatment.
    - **Conservative**: 40,000 extra police; 10-fold rise in drug rehab places; addicts to choose rehab or prison; end some early releases; 20,000 more prison places; judges to set minimum and maximum sentences.
    - **Liberal Democrat**: 10,000 extra police; tackle drug dealers rather than cannabis users; out-of-hours school courses against 'yob' culture; local communities to decide sentences for low-level criminals.

  (Holyrood 2007)
    - **Labour**: retain DNA and fingerprints of all crime suspects; justice centres to allow criminals to carry out 'pay back' duties in communities.
    - **Conservative**: more police officers; additional investment in drug rehab services; judges to be given discretion to refuse bail/review operation of bail.
    - **Liberal Democrat**: more police; tougher community services with offenders working to repay crimes; youth justice boards.
    - **SNP**: extra police; end short term jail sentences; more info for communities on dangerous paedophiles in their area.

- *Education*
  (Westminster 2005)
    - **Labour**: parents can select specialist schools; 200 new City Academies; new powers to control truancy and disruption; university top-up fees up to £3,000, with grants for poorest students.
    - **Conservative**: 600,000 new school places to boost choice; allow good schools to expand and create new ones; heads able to expel disruptive pupils; no student fees - charge interest on loans.
    - **Liberal Democrat**: cut class sizes for youngest children; all children to be taught by a qualified teacher in each subject; abolish 'unnecessary tests'; scrap university fees.

  (Holyrood 2007)
    - **Labour**: leaving school at 16/17 conditional on being in EE&T; create skills academies; literacy and arithmetic tests for school leavers.
    - **Conservative**: more power to head teachers; councils to be given control of education budgets.
    - **Liberal Democrat**: new schools. Extra teachers; reduce class sizes; one hour physical activity per child per day.
    - **SNP**: abolish graduate endowment and pay off graduate debt; cut class size to 18 in P1-P3.
- *Taxation*
  (Westminster 2005)
    - **Labour**: reform the 'unsustainable' council tax; spending plans affordable without tax rises; tax relief for 'hard working families'.
    - **Conservative**: no 'Third Term' tax rises; £4bn to cut taxes including £1.3bn cut in council tax for pensioners; possible cuts to inheritance tax and stamp duty.
    - **Liberal Democrat**: replace council tax with a local income tax; new 50% tax rate on earnings over £100,000 a year; raise stamp duty threshold to £150,000 to help first-time buyers.

  (Holyrood 2007)
    - **Labour**: no above inflation Council Tax increases.
    - **Conservative**: retain Council Tax with 50% cut for all households where occupants over 65.
    - **Liberal Democrat**: abolish Council Tax and set Local Income Tax from 2009-2010 (average rate 3.5% to 3.75%.)
    - **SNP**: abolish Council Tax and set Local Income Tax nationwide at 3p (at basic and higher rates.)
- EU (Westminster 2007)
    - **Labour**: adoption of proposed EU constitution after referendum; join the single currency if five economic tests show it is in UK interests; UK should be at 'heart' of Europe.
    - **Conservative**: opposed to EU constitution and would hold early vote; UK to get powers back over fishing; quit the social chapter; oppose adopting euro.
    - **Liberal Democrat**: Work towards the right conditions for joining the euro, then call referendum; pro EU constitution.
- In 2004 Michael Howard complained that New Labour was stealing every Conservative policy within days of it being unveiled; now accused of stealing Conservative policies on inheritance and 'non-dom' taxes and Lib. Dem policy of taxing air travel.
- Heavy prison sentences originally Conservative Party Policy.
- Both Conservative and Labour vying to be seen as the more competent administrators of a free market economy.
- Conservative admission that there will be no tax reductions during any first term in office.
- Issue of 'green taxation'.
- Absence of real differences seen as a significant cause of fall in election turnout.
- Other relevant points.

Study Theme 1D: Electoral Systems, Voting and Political Attitudes

Question A4

"Pass" and better answers should feature developed, exemplified knowledge and understanding of:
- The influence of social class on voting behaviour
- The influence of other factors on voting behaviour

and
- Balanced comment on/analysis of the influence of social class on voting behaviour.

Answers may refer to:
- various measures of social class: Register General's Social Scale, Standard Occupational Classification. The National Socio-Economic Classification Standard and links to voting behaviour.

- party support across social class seems to have continued along traditional lines; support was highest for the Conservatives in the top AB class and for Labour in the lower cohorts.
- Conservatives retained the largest share of AB vote and C1 vote. Share of C2 and DE rose from 2001 to 2005.
- Labour had the largest share of C2 and DE vote (but both fell).
- the Liberal Democrats increased their share in each group between 2001 and 2005.
- Labour has made long-term gains in the AB and C1 voters.
- Conservative lead over Labour in the ABC's down from 35% between 1974 and 1992 to 5% or less in the 1997, 2001 and 2005 elections.
- importance attached by political parties/ psephologists to sub-groups within social classes: Mondeo Man/Worcester Woman/ School Gate Mums.
- class dealignment - evidence that the electorate less committed (more floating voters) than in the past.
- Labour and Conservatives have won elections because they have been able to attract the support of people outside their core groups. While social class remains a strong indicator of party loyalty, social-economic divisions are much more complex than they used to be.
- Conservatives gained support amongst DE voters between 1997 and 2005.
- Labour gained support amongst AB voters between 1997 and 2005.
- changing nature of class.
- extent to which parties have abandoned their traditional ideological positions.
- in Scotland, different parties are in competition in socially similar areas. The electorate is aware of this and hence people of similar social backgrounds vote for different parties in different constituencies.
- the Rational Choice Model includes factors such as current issues, party leaders, past performance.
- the nature of the election, its importance, the workings of the electoral system being used are also now taken into account.
- Liberal Democrats did especially well in constituencies where there was a particular reason why voters might be disenchanted with Labour; those with large numbers of Muslim voters and those with large student populations.
- the Labour Party vote fell on average by over 5% more in seats with a relatively large Muslim population than it did in those with little or no such population. The increase in the Liberal Democrat vote meanwhile was around 5 points in such seats.
- the Labour Party vote fell by around 3% more in constituencies with large numbers of students, to the apparent benefit of the Liberal Democrat Party.
- the Green Party's best share of the vote (4.5%) came in constituencies where over 30% adults have a degree.
- the BNP did best in constituencies with relatively low proportions of people with a degree, especially if the constituency had a relatively large number of Muslims.
- UKIP did best in constituencies with a relatively large number of older people and, in places with few voters with degrees.
- Labour continues to be strong in its traditional heartlands in Scotland, Wales and the North of England. The Conservatives in the East and the South. Only in the South West did the Liberal Democrats secure 40% or more. In geographic terms, Scotland and Wales remain central to any Labour majority.
- no Conservative MPs in the big cities such as Birmingham, Manchester, Liverpool, Leeds, Sheffield and Glasgow.
- although gender appeared to have had little influence on party preference (34% of men and 38% women voted Labour) - 34/32 for Conservatives - there was a lower swing to the Conservatives among women (1.5%) than among men (5%).
- research claims that turnout increases by 4% in constituencies contested by women.
- among those in the 18-34 age group, 38% voted Labour, 27% Liberal Democrat and 21% Conservative.
- evidence suggests that it is no longer the case that people become significantly more inclined to vote, as they grow older.
- more than 81% of successful candidates served in the previous Parliament and only 18% elected for the first time.
- other relevant points.

Section B – Social Issues in the United Kingdom

Study Theme 2: Wealth and Health Inequalities in the United Kingdom

Question B5

"Pass" and better answers should feature developed, exemplified knowledge and understanding of:
- Government policies to reduce gender and ethnic inequalities
- The impact of government policies on gender and ethnic inequalities

and
- Balanced comment on/analysis of the effectiveness of government policies to reduce inequalities.

Answers may refer to:
- Child Tax Credit and Working Tax Credit.
- Government sees affordable child care as crucial to narrowing the wage gap.
- Minimum Wage and Statutory Pay Obligations.
- Maternity and Paternity leave.
- since 2003 companies have had to give serious consideration to employees (both genders) with children under six who request flexible working hours: one in five working women and one in ten men have taken up this 'right to request'.
- Skills Strategy (July 2003) to address the fact that over 50% of women in part time work are working below their skill level.
- 2004: government set new Public Services Agreement targets for under-represented groups in senior management (two of which relate to women) for 2008.
- Equality Act (2006).
- Women's Enterprise Task Force.
- Work and Families Act (2006) extended the right to request flexible working.
- Gender Equality Duty Code of Practice (from April 2007) places legal responsibility on public authorities to demonstrate that they treat men and women fairly. (Implications for delivery of health care to both genders.)
- Public Service Agreement Targets:
  - 37% women in the Senior Civil Service (SCS);
  - 30% women in top management posts (Pay Bands 2&3);
  - 4% ethnic minority staff in the SCS;
- the Commission for Equality and Human Rights (2007).
- Race Relations (Amendment) Act, 2000.
- Ethnic Minority Employment Task Force (2004) to tackle unemployment among black and Asian people.
- Education and Training policies.
- One Scotland.
- strategic review of local race equality work in Scotland (2004).
- gender pay gap between 2005 and 2006 at its lowest value since records began.

- women now make up 60% of the university population.
- success of women in reaching senior posts varies from place to place. Glass ceiling only cracked, not broken.
- women make up 46% of all millionaires and are expected to own 60% of the UK's wealth by 2010.
- EOC research shows women make up less than 10% of the senior judiciary, senior police officers, top business leaders, national newspaper editors and 0.8% of senior ranks in the armed forces, despite accounting for over half of the UK population and 46% of the labour force.
- higher women rise up the pay ladder, the greater pay gap becomes; 23% at director level.
- gender pay gap: UK women in full time work earn 17% less per hour than men. (New laws urgently needed to tackle this according to EOC recommendation, September 2007.)
- pay gap higher in the private sector than in the public sector.
- 155% increase in equal pay cases being lodged with tribunals between 2006-2007.
- occupational segregation: 70% of women with qualifications in science, engineering and technology do not work in those professions.
- state pension not 'gender proofed'.
- 'wraparound' state childcare policy, from 8am to 6pm unlikely to be in place before 2010.
- women from Black Caribbean, Pakistani and Bangladeshi groups (despite 'stellar' GSCE performance), likely to face a higher risk of unemployment, lower pay and fewer prospects for promotion.
- the CRE says that local government and the criminal justice system (including the police) have made good progress. However Whitehall departments, NHS trusts, further education colleges, district council and the Olympic Delivery Authority have fallen short.
- whereas there are 3,460 white members of the senior civil service, only 70 are Asian and 20 black. Overall, just 4.1% of the top ranks come from a black or minority ethnic background.
- a study by the Joseph Rowntree Foundation, reveals that ethnic minorities suffer twice the level of poverty of white Britons, as discrimination and disadvantage blight their life chances.
- the study finds that many Pakistanis and Bangladeshis are paid so little they are still classed as poor. 'Income poverty' traps 1 in 9 whites, but 6 out of 10 Bangladeshis, 4 out of 10 Pakistanis and 3 out of 10 Britons of black African heritage.
- "We have helped an additional quarter of a million people from ethnic minorities move into work over the last few years and the employment rate has risen to 60% in the last three years. But we are aware that more needs to be done." (Jim Murphy former minister for employment and welfare reform).
- other relevant points.

Question B6

"Pass" and better answers should feature developed, exemplified knowledge and understanding of:
- the *collectivist* and *individualist* approaches to health care and welfare provision policies
- Government health and welfare provision policies

and
- Balanced comment on/analysis of the view that government, not individuals, should be responsible for health care and welfare provision.

Answers may refer to:
- Collectivist emphasis on responsibility of government to invest in health and welfare to counteract inequalities borne by those who are victims of an exploitive system.
- original Beveridge principles of the welfare state; funded by social insurance and taxation, with citizens being provided for 'from cradle to grave', specifically with regards to health, housing, employment, education and poverty.
- public health care should be funded from taxation.
- Individualist emphasis on a reduced role for government, 'lifestyle choices' and greater individual responsibility.
- view that there is no such thing as society, only individuals.
- individuals should provide for their own health care through the private sector.
- view that the collectivist approach encourages a 'dependency culture'.
- affordability of the welfare state dependent on getting even more people off benefit and into work.
- link between unemployment among lone parents and child poverty.
- Labour's 'Third Way' - the welfare state exists for those in genuine need, but individuals have to be encouraged to become more self-sufficient.
- promotion of 'social inclusion' through 'welfare to work' policies with private sector involvement.
- welfare provision governed by 'rights and responsibilities'/'a hand up, not a hand out'.
- targeting and means - testing of benefits.
- Government response to the Turner Report on pensions.
- proposals for benefit reform.
- NHS continues to be supported from taxation; with mainstream clinical services staying public but the advantages of private sector involvement to meet targets is welcomed (less so in Scotland when Labour administered).
- emphasis on 'healthy lifestyles'.
- Labour's 'holistic' approach to health and welfare: health is not seen in isolation - its relationship to social class is acknowledged.
- Government has achieved success in lowering unemployment but there are still concerns about the high number of, for example, IB claimants.
- the numbers in absolute poverty have gone down, but relative poverty has increased as the income gap between rich and poor has widened.
- health inequalities still a cause for concern.
- other relevant points.

Section C - International Issues

Study Theme 3A: The Republic of South Africa

Question C7

"Pass" and better answers should feature developed, exemplified knowledge and understanding of:
- The main aims and features of Black Economic Empowerment
- The impact of Black Economic Empowerment on reducing inequalities

and
- Balanced comment on/analysis of the effectiveness of BEE in reducing economic inequalities.

Answers may refer to:
- BEE originally seen as a broad-based government strategy that would transfer economic power to Blacks without disrupting the SA economy.
- BEE applies to skill, education and know-how as well as business.
- 1998 Employment Equity Act aimed at ensuring black South Africans get preferential treatment in hiring, promotion, university admission and the awarding of government contracts.
- 2004 BEE legislation contained more rigorous affirmative action.

- BEE Codes of Good Practice 2007 (to be reviewed in 10 years), involve transferring ownership to black people and women, ensuring representation at board and management level and preferential procurement of goods and services from black- and female-owned enterprises: setting of ambitious targets within 10-15 years.
- introduction of 'generic score cards' 55 of the 100 points focused on workers and those unlikely to have a shareholding in the company.
- many of BEE's voluntarily agreed targets are modest and not all are expected to be achieved.
- BEE Advisory Council advises on and reviews BEE with aims of identifying sectors/ stakeholders in economy that are BEE compliant.
- BEE mandatory only for government and state-owned companies but BEE credentials pretty much required for those wishing to do business with the state.
- less than 2% of companies (accounting for 61% of the GDP) have to wrestle with the full codes. Foreign companies exempted from some of the rules.
- first informal phase of BEE saw it appointing party loyalists to senior posts in state corporations and using them as training grounds for future capitalists and managers.
- in 2004 - 68% BEE deals went to 6 black-owned (top ANC members') businesses.
- growing and diversifying black middle class. BUPPIES (black and up and coming professionals) comprise 2.6 million 'black diamonds' - a 30% increase in less than two years.
- Anglo-American appointed its first black CEO in 2005.
- Patrice Motsepe - first black South African to make it to the Forbes Billionaires List (2008).
- 7% of the Stock Exchange ownership has moved into black hands (target 25%).
- whites control 90% of the assets and big companies.
- most companies nowhere near target of 40% black managers.
- many black businesses have failed or are struggling but successful black-owned businesses are now part of everyday life.
- pace of BEE varies from region to region. Progress slower in Kwa Zulu-Natal than in other areas.
- many BEE deals said to collapse into cronyism and corruption.
- except for a minority of instant millionaires, the majority of black people remain on the edges of the economy.
- income differentials between blacks and whites have declined.
- number of wealthy black households has increased far more quickly than whites.
- low income black households have dropped but whites have risen.
- whites total income share has fallen but blacks has risen.

BUT
- increase in number of people in shanty towns (5 toilets between 7000 people in Foreman Road).
- only 5% blacks obtaining university entrance qualifications.
- as high as 77% of children in the best state performing schools are white.
- among the unemployed, 52% of blacks have no access to a regular wage earner.
- half of the local authority areas do not provide sanitation, clean water or rubbish collection to more than 40% of their households.
- 2m families live in shacks with no running water.
- whites have higher proportion of skilled or very skilled employment.
- skills deficit very much in evidence - South Africa had to import 2000 workers from Taiwan to build a new SASOL plant.
- 4·5m unemployed and an additional 3·5m who have given up looking for a job.
- 80% of unemployed aged between 15-34.
- 4m living on less than $1 a day (2m in 1994).
- two thirds of South Africa's income held by a (mostly white) top 20%.
- view that BEE is about the transfer, not the transformation of power. It has turned South African into a 'cappuccino' society: a lot of black coffee at the bottom, a layer of white foam on top and a sprinkling of cocoa on the very top for show. This has neither led to a wider distribution of wealth nor to a greater opening up of opportunities for previously disadvantaged individuals.
- view that BEE is disempowerment for whites and Asians.
- other relevant points.

Study Theme 3B: The People's Republic of China

Question C8

"Pass" and better answers should feature developed, exemplified knowledge and understanding of:
- Evidence of 'democracy' in China.
- The 'undemocratic' features of Chinese society.

and
- Balanced comment on/analysis of the extent to which China is becoming a more democratic society.

Answers may refer to:
- constitution guarantees the fundamental rights of all citizens, including freedom of speech.
- in March 1999, the National People's Congress (NPC) included the concept of rule of law into China's constitution.
- more open reporting of issues of concern in the media.
- political reform officially on the CPC agenda and is being introduced from the bottom up.
- contested elections in villages every three years since 1988, but these are controlled by the CPC through the selection/monitoring of candidates; direct elections at village and more recently township level are by law supposed to be free but local officials are thought to interfere/ manipulate; evidence of arrests of villagers/ lawyers who protest about selection process/ results.
- talk of elections at county level and perhaps higher.
- Hong Kong (since 1997): half of government is non-communist and democratically elected although the leader is appointee of the CPC; free press, freedom of association, etc.
- 2007 saw first ever contest in the election (chosen by committee of 800 pro-Beijing 'voters') for the chief executive of Hong Kong - winner had to put on a show of electioneering.
- reform of the legal system in response to the market economy.
- in 2006 the Supreme Court reclaimed the power to review all death sentences.
- dissidents allowed to funeral service of deposed party chief Zhao Ziyang in 2005 and in November 2006 CPC organised a public commemoration of the 90th anniversary of the late Hu Yaoang, ousted because of reformist beliefs.
- widening of CPC membership to private business people who make up one third of membership but this is seen more as a pragmatic move to support business and not to extend democracy.
- anonymous text message on mobile phones prompted inhabitants of Xiamen to join one of the biggest middle class protests of recent years (May 2007). Protest (successful) was against plans to build huge chemical factory on a site in the suburbs.

- China remains a one party state with the Communist Party of China (CPC) in overall control.
- CPC controls the government by screening appointments and promotions to all posts: all appointments must be approved by the level above; there are elections to local and national congresses but direct election only at the lowest level.
- Organised opposition to CPC banned.
- CPC's power not as great as in earlier years; weakened by fiscal and administrative decentralisation but CPC continues to control the overall direction of policy.
- report on Building of Political Democracy in China 2005 stressed the continued rule of the CPC. 'Democracy' in CPC speak does not mean allowing organised opposition.
- CPC does not allow free speech, a free media or organised protests but more grassroots organisations/activities beginning to develop; CPC tries to manage those who threaten indirectly and suppress those who challenge directly.
- Reporters Without Borders (RSF) rates China 163/167 in the world for press freedom.
- outspoken newspapers or editors sacked. *Bing Dian* closed in 2006 reputedly as part of a long-nurtured scheme to silence the paper's "pursuit of democracy, rule of law, deliberation, liberty and rights", according to its editor.
- high number of imprisoned journalists - 31 in 2006.
- Police force of 30,000 on-line monitors - dissidents who net-post views are imprisoned.
- evidence of lengthy detentions without trial for dissidents.
- no open elections in Hong Kong before 2017 and all candidates will have to be approved by central government. 2020 at earliest before Hong Kong citizens will have the right to directly elect all members of the city's legislature.
- crackdown on Falun Gong.
- events in Xinjiang and Tibet.
- other relevant points.

Study Theme 3C: The United States of America

Question C9

"Pass" and better answers should feature developed, exemplified knowledge and understanding of:
- The powers of the President of the United States of America
- The ways in which Congress and the Supreme Court can check the powers of the President

and
- Balanced comment on/analysis of the effectiveness of Congress and the Supreme Court in checking the powers of the President.

Answers may refer to:
- powers of the President laid out in the Constitution.
- Chief ambassador - determines foreign policy and diplomacy; appoints ambassadors and diplomats.
- may propose legislation at any time; calling a press conference; making an announcement at a public event.
- can issue rules/regulations and instructions (Executive Orders)* that have the force of law and do not need Congressional approval *but may be declared unconstitutional by the Supreme Court.* (*173 in Bush's first term).
- submits the budget to Congress.
- signs legislation; can refuse to release money for legislation that he disapproves.
- President can issue 'signing statements' in which he gives directions about the ways in which legislation should be understood and interpreted.
- can adjourn/recall Congress *but Congress does not have to pass any laws during special sessions.*
- may veto legislation. Must act within ten congressional working days of receiving a bill from Congress. Only vetoes bills he is likely to be unsuccessfully challenged on (always studies final passage votes). In 2001-5, Bush was the first president since 1841 to get through an entire 4-year term without using a veto.
- Bush's first use of the veto was in July 2006 (Stem Cell Research Enhancement Act). *A two-thirds majority vote in both the Senate and the House can override a veto as was the case in November 2007 (a bill authorising spending on water projects) - the first successful overturning of a presidential veto since 1998.*
- for a brief period between 1997 and 1998 Clinton had the 'line item veto' power *until the Supreme Court declared it unconstitutional.*
- 'pocket' veto can be used only at the end of a congressional session. *Congress cannot override.*
- runs the executive branch of the federal government and nominates executive branch officials and all federal judges (including the 9 Supreme Court Judges). *Senate confirms appointments by simple majority vote.*
- may make a 'recess appointment'. Bush's recess appointment of John Bolton as US ambassador to the UN bypassed the need for Senate confirmation.
- acts as Commander in Chief of armed forces (has power to wage war while constitutionally Congress declares and funds it); may call out the National Guard.
- In 2002 Bush claimed an inherent presidential authority to order military actions to pre-empt hostile action against the USA. What constitutes a threat is at the discretion of the president.
- Negotiates treaties. *Congress scrutinises and a 2/3 Senate majority is required for ratification.*
- in 2007 Bush lost the power to negotiate trade deals without Congressional backing.
- may commute a sentence (commuted Lewis 'Scooter' Libby's 30 month prison sentence in 2007) and issue a pardon at any time, even before a crime is charged, *but the power to grant pardon does not extend to impeachment.*
- appoints the Executive Office of the President.
- may make 'personal interventions' and issue 'statements'. When a Bill banning the 'cruel, inhuman and degrading treatment of detainees by Americans anywhere in the world' was signed, a statement was issued reserving the right of the President to flout it.
- the House of Representatives may impeach the President. Senate conducts the trial. *(Speaker Pelosi has made it clear that impeachment proceedings against either the Vice-President or the President are "off the table").*
- Legislative and nominee filibusters.
- Supreme Court can declare the actions of any member of the executive branch, including the President, to be unconstitutional. (Judicial Review).
- when the Supreme Court ruled that Mr Bush had exceeded his authority in setting up, without congressional approval, special military commissions to try some of the Guantanamo detainees, the President pushed through the 2006 Military Commission Act giving him just such authority.
- Terry Schiavo case (2005).
- resignation of US attorney general Alberto Gonzales seen as a congressional 'scalp'.
- President often referred to as 'bargainer-in-chief.
- No Child Left Behind legislation passed with bipartisan support because the Democrats liked the extra money Bush threw in to sweeten the deal.
- Bush's reform plans for social security failed - as did those on immigration (but was able to end 'catch and release' via an address to the nation).

- Bush found it difficult to get bills through Congress (even before Democratic 2006 mid-term elections successes) because of divisions in his own party.
- presidential power traditionally thrives in emergency and crisis conditions.
- claim that Bush has marginalised Congress and established an 'imperial presidency'.
- second term Presidents seen as 'lame ducks'.
- other relevant points.

Study Theme 3D: The European Union

Question C10

"Pass" and better answers should feature developed, exemplified knowledge and understanding of:
- The positive consequences of enlargement
- Concerns over recent and possible future enlargement

and
- Balanced comment on/analysis of the impact of enlargement on the EU.

Answers may refer to:
- increase from 15 to 25 members in 2004, to 27 in 2007.
- Romania and Bulgaria became the 26th and 27th members at start of 2007.
- Croatia is engaged in formal membership talks. Macedonia has achieved candidate status and others are waiting in the wings.
- the Copenhagen criteria for membership include democracy, a free market economy, observance of human and minority rights, and political stability.
- stronger, peaceful and more stable Europe - lead up to membership has stimulated a wide range of social and economic reforms in new member states.
- has further promoted the rule of law and respect for human rights in new democracies.
- has helped the east European countries as they moved from communist central planning to liberal democracy.
- a more influential voice in international affairs.
- countries of western Balkans have been pacified and stabilised after the bloody 1990s thanks mainly to their hopes of EU membership.
- weakens Franco-German domination.
- opportunities for business.
- cheap labour good for economies of richer members.
- UK, Ireland and Swedish economies said to have gained the most. (They immediately fully opened their labour markets to workers from the new entrants.)
- closer cooperation in dealing with crime.
- changes made in Turkey to boost hopes of membership.
- French and Dutch rejections of the constitution in 2005 partly reflected dissatisfaction over the 2004 enlargement.
- fears that EU machinery, originally designed for 6 members, cannot function effectively with 30 or more members.
- the *widening* (admitting new members) as against *deepening* (further integration of new members) dispute.
- impact on decision-making procedures - each member has veto on foreign policy making.
- relocation of business to countries with lower labour costs and worse social protection.
- immigration control issues.
- implications of extension of Schengen Agreement, which allows people to cross borders without having their passports checked, to 25 members (not UK and Ireland).
- demands on structural funds; losers and winners in development aid stakes.
- budgetary issues - UK rebate; CAP reform (or lack of it).
- new members likely to resist initiatives that cost more than they can easily afford.
- concerns about some new members being too pro-USA and too quick to provoke Russia.
- Poland the only member to block the start of negotiations with Russia on a new partnership agreement.
- Polish threat to veto any alteration to voting rights.
- many measures judged necessary to ensure that the enlarged union could continue to function put on hold by EU constitution stalling in 2005 after referendum defeats in France and Holland.
- Nice Treaty can only function in a union of 27 members maximum – no more can join until a new treaty is in place.
- UK and Denmark now joined by Poland, Hungary and the Czech Republic as non-euro members.
- Turkey accepted as eligible in 1963. If it ever joins it could become the most populous member by 2020 with more voting weight and more European Members than Germany.
- David Milliband's suggestion that the EU should expand beyond Europe to Russia, Middle East and Africa.
- implications of the Lisbon Treaty.
- enlargement brings economic benefits, cements political stability in Eastern Europe and lessens the prospects of a federal Europe.
- other relevant points.

Study Theme 3E: The Politics of Developments in Africa

Question C11

"Pass" and better answers should feature developed, exemplified knowledge and understanding with reference to specific African countries (excluding the Republic of South Africa) of:
- The role of education and health care in development
- Other factors that contribute to development

and
- Balanced comment on/analysis of the importance of education and health care to successful development.

Answers may refer to:
- education and health care provision (neither widely available free of charge in Africa), seen as fundamental to a country's economic and social development.
- impact of literacy levels, school enrolment, levels of expenditure on health and education (public and private) in both actual and percentage terms, life expectancy, and infant/child mortality rates on development.
- lack of properly trained teachers, overcrowded classrooms, lack of teaching resources.
- African countries cannot afford to fund free health care. Health care professionals attracted by conditions in more developed nations.
- impact of HIV/AIDS and malaria.
- initiatives to eradicate extreme poverty and hunger/empower women/make cash available to encourage local businesses (on average it takes 64 days to register a business in Africa).
- importance of property rights and the rule of law.
- impact of other factors on development: good governance, conflict, debt, aid (and its uses), international investment, globalisation, types and levels of a country's natural resources.
- Millennium Project has set up 12 'research villages' (target of 1000 by 2009) in 10 African countries to pioneer models of development (The Magnificent Seven) that can be copied but there is an admission that successful implementation depends upon foreign aid.
- even when aid is 'properly' used, development does not come overnight: when Zambia's foreign debt was reduced; most of the savings were spent on recruiting teachers and improving health care (fees for basic health care removed). Nevertheless, Zambia remains poor and still depends on aid.

- Mali is one of only five African countries to have fully qualified for America's Millennium Challenge Account with its stringent criteria for good governance.
- Niger is the second poorest country on the planet but it is a democracy and has a free press. There has been a very slow response to its problems.
- according to the IMF, Africa's economy is growing steadily but this masks differences between countries whose economies are improving (in many cases those rich in natural resources) and those, like Zimbabwe, and more recently, Kenya, whose are going backwards.
- similarly, there are development differences within specific countries. (Sudan has an oil-rich but undeveloped south complementing an educated, commercial north with few natural resources). Northern government feels no obligation either to share its wealth with poorer peripheral provinces or to behave well towards them.
- recognition by **both** the UN Investing in Development: A Practical Plan to achieve the Millennium Goals **and** the Commission For Africa that "more aid is needed to meet Africa's development needs". However "outsiders cannot deliver development, it must be done by Africans" (Commission for Africa report).
- Africa's population continues to increase with nothing like the required rate of economic growth to sustain it. Population growth has been described as the 'unmentionable', the elephant in the corner of the room.
- other relevant points.

Study Theme 3F: Global Security

Question C12

"Pass" and better answers should feature developed, exemplified knowledge and understanding of:
- The part played by the USA in achieving global security
- Concerns about the part played by the USA in achieving global security

and
- Balanced comment on/analysis of the part played by the USA in achieving global security.

Answers may refer to:
- significance of both UN and NATO membership.
- spends the most money on UN peacekeeping. Pays about 26% of the cost for UN peacekeeping missions - size of contribution limited by US domestic law.
- has frequently led demands for reform of the UN, hinting that otherwise its financial contribution may fail.
- support crucial to election of Ban Ki Moon as UN Secretary General. View that the USA supported a weak candidate in order to undermine an organisation with which it has always had problems.
- provides 0·5% of UN peacekeeping personnel - president retains command of military personnel.
- view that without strong US leadership and involvement the UN would not amount to much and there is no hope of a peaceful and stable future for humanity this century.
- gives protection to NATO and strongly supports the NATO Response Force.
- preferred to act alone after 9/11 despite NATO invoking Article 5 of its treaty - an attack on one ally is an attack on all.
- chose allied units in coalitions of the willing to go to war (on terror) in Afghanistan.
- protracted US/NATO difficulties in Afghanistan, where Americans bear the brunt of the fighting.
- invasion of Iraq in 2003, led by USA and UK (opposed by France and Germany): consequences for long-term peace and security in the area.
- NATO as a whole declined to send troops to Iraq (apart from a small training mission) but eventually agreed to take over ISAF (International Security Assistance Force) in Afghanistan.
- Taliban and Saddam Hussein speedily toppled from power but war on terror has since appeared to go less well.
- US forces retain responsibility for hunting down al-Qaeda's fugitive figurehead Osama Bin Laden.
- relentless US diplomatic pressure to secure peace in the Middle East (Road Map); pressure on Israel to withdraw from Lebanon.
- USA-led Proliferation Security Initiative as a response to concerns over spread of WMD.
- 2007 Creation of AFRICOM (U.S Africa Command).
- USA played a big role in ending the war between north and south Sudan but the UN's failure to stop either the atrocities in Darfur or the nuclear posturing of Iran and North Korea has stemmed largely from the inability of the so-called P5 (of which the USA is one) to agree on what should be done.
- USA opposed the Ethiopian invasion of Somalia in 2006 to topple the Union of Islamic Courts but gave assistance after the event.
- October 2007 sanctions against Iran seen as a reflection of USA's despair at the UN.
- Russia blames US push for eastward expansion of NATO and US support for groups that have toppled governments in the former Soviet sphere of influence for increased tension.
- USA's missile defence plans for Europe seen as a threat to global security by Russia - USA accused of reigniting the arms race. Russia has threatened to place missiles in Belarus and has halted its participation in the Conventional Forces in Europe Treaty.
- US policy towards North Korea and Iran (axis of evil), has heightened tension but could be seen to reduce nuclear proliferation and through joint diplomacy with others, has secured agreement for North Korea/Iran not to develop weapons-grade nuclear material.
- USA (has positioned the 2nd aircraft carrier group in the Gulf) seen as being on a collision course with Iran which it accuses of support for insurgents in Iraq and over Iran's continued attempts to develop regional supremacy.
- USA rejected the International Landmine Treaty.
- USA has given immunity to US subjects involved in actions to combat terrorism.
- accusations that the USA is a major arms supplier worldwide.
- Americans emphasise counter-terrorism and counter-insurgency.
- Europeans are more comfortable with peacekeeping and stabilisation.
- USA is in a position to play a decisive role in achieving global security - given its military, economic and technological capabilities - but it has always had a tendency towards unilateralism.
- other relevant points.

MODERN STUDIES HIGHER
PAPER 2
2008

1. Daphne Millar claims: "*The most common reasons for not handing in a prescription are to do with cost [or the price per item is such that many adults find it very difficult to pay]* **and** *no-one finds that they did not need it after all.*"
   Source C1*(a)* shows that 28% of people didn't hand in prescriptions because it cost less to buy the medicine over the counter, while 25% didn't hand it in because it cost too much money. However 10% of people said that their health improved - did not need it after all.

2. (*a*) Daphne Millar claims: "*Free prescriptions would make a huge difference as to whether patients did or did not go to their doctor.*"
   Source C1*(b)* shows just over 10% would be much more likely to go/it would make no difference to almost 80%.

   (*b*) Tom Beattie claims: "*In a recent survey on health care systems in European countries, the UK was one of the highest rated.*"
   Source C2 shows that 7 out of the 11 countries had their health care systems rated/scored higher than the UK.

3. Tom Beattie claims: "*Most people who have to can afford to pay for all the items on their prescriptions and there is little support from health and community groups for completely abolishing prescription charges.*"
   Source C1*(c)* shows that more than 60% can afford all of the items but Source C3 shows 50% support for abolishing prescription charges.

4. **Credit:**
   A style appropriate to a report (sub-headings, chapters etc) with:
   - an introduction that indicates an awareness of the role to be adopted and makes a clear recommendation
   - developed arguments in support of the recommendation
   - identification of and comment on (rebuttal of) counter arguments
   - synthesis of source information
   - provision and use of appropriate background knowledge
   - an overall conclusion.

   Arguments for the proposal may feature:
   - charges may lead to suffering and poorer health
   - experience in Wales
   - effects of cost especially on lower income groups
   - long term damage to health when prescriptions not taken up
   - evidence from GPs
   - costs relative to overall NHS budget
   - impracticality of lump sum payments

   Arguments against the proposal may feature:
   - spiralling cost of drugs
   - exemptions already protect the poor/children/elderly
   - option of buying over the counter
   - charges discourage time wasters coming to surgeries
   - adverse effect on the provision of new drugs
   - benefits will be for the better off not the poor
   - will lead to cutbacks elsewhere that will worsen the health gap

   Credit background knowledge-based argument developed from references in:

   Source A
   - The Scottish Government......... phase out and eventually abolish... charges
   - the effects on individuals and in the longer term on the NHS
   - the founding principles of the NHS
   - an immediate improvement in the health of the nation

   Source B
   - the rising costs of medicines
   - the NHS has... enjoyed public support
   - the financing and performance of the NHS in Scotland
   - If the health gap is to be closed

   Other background knowledge-based argument may include:
   - the extent and causes of ill health
   - the extent of poverty
   - foreign comparisons
   - recent media coverage
   - relevant personal experiences
   - other relevant points

MODERN STUDIES HIGHER
PAPER 1
2009

Section A – Political Issues in the United Kingdom

Study Theme 1A – Devolved Decision Making in Scotland

Question A1

"Pass" and better answers should feature developed, exemplified knowledge and understanding of:
The impact of the devolved powers on decision making for Scotland.
The impact of other feaures of devolution on decision making for Scotland.
And
Balanced comment on/analysis of the impact of devolution on decision making in Scotland.

Answers may refer to:

The devolved powers.
- Provide the opportunity to deliver "Scottish solutions to Scottish problems."
- Legislation enacted by the Scottish parliament that would have been unlikely to be passed within the time constraints imposed at Westminster.
- Criticisms made of "waste of time legislation": the Fur Farming (Prohibition) Scotland Bill – Scotland didn't have any fur farms. The Anti-Social Behaviour Bill of 2004 aimed at cutting youth crime but it increased; view that things have not even improved for foxes, with more killed after abolition than before.
- Criticisms that debates often staged on matters over which the Scottish Parliament has no control, for example, identity cards.

The reserved powers
- Disputes arising from these: nuclear power, extradition of Libyan prisoners, control over elections, financial help to scrap council tax and fund free personal care, share of Westminster funding for English prison building, immigration and asylum (Vucaj case).
- "Barnett Formula" funding levels for Scotland.
- Sewel Motions (instances when it is convenient for legislation on devolved matters to be passed by the UK Parliament).
- Retention by Westminster of responsibility for fiscal and monetary policy leaves the Scottish parliament impotent in the face of world economic and financial crisis.

The electoral system
- Significance of same/different party-led governments at Holyrood and Westminster.
- Resulting coalition and minority led governments have been criticised as being "legislation light" (in the SNP's first year of government, nine bills were introduced of which five passed).
- View that the Scottish Parliament has been used more as a forum of debate with the First Minister governing outside it by executive order (reversal of hospital closures, reduction in prescription charges) – "relying on the strength of argument in parliament, not the argument of parliamentary strength".
- Concern that little or no progress has been made on a number of pledges in the SNP 2007 election manifesto.
- The role of the Joint Ministerial Committees.
- View that the respective roles of the Scotland Office, Scottish Secretary and (reduced number of) Scottish MPs at Westminster are being marginalised.
- 2002 survey findings that 48% of councillors thought that devolution had reduced the role of local government.
- Calman Commission interim report (December 2008) made no recommendations about extending devolution.
- Other relevant points.

Study Theme 1B – Decision Making in Central Government

Question A2

"Pass" and better answers should feature developed, exemplified knowledge and understanding of:
The opportunities for and ways in which backbench MPs may influence decision making in Central Government.
The limitations on the opportunities and ways in which backbench MPs may influence decision making in Central Government.
And
Balanced comment on/analysis of the view that backbench MPs have little influence on decision making in Central Government.

Answers may refer to:
- Opportunities for backbench MPs to influence decision making in central government include debates, select committees, standing committees, House of Commons inquiries, Ministerial Question Time, Prime Minister Question Time, liaison committee, early day motions, Ten Minute Rule Bills, Private Members Bills, Opposition days, Parliamentary Party groups and divisions.
- Ministers see questions in advance although supplementary questions are allowed.
- Prime Ministers questions not seen in advance but no supplementary questions are allowed.
- MPs can write to the speaker indicating a desire to speak in debate but no guarantee that they will be called.
- Standing committees (which scrutinise every new law) are thinly attended and skip over chunks of each bill.
- MPs don't have the time to look at legislation in detail – have to put more energy into their constituency work if they want to get re-elected.
- "Influence" limited by the whip system, the executive's control of the parliamentary timetable and the payroll vote.
- The Government controls the legislative timetable.
- Tony Blair's first ever defeat came in 2005 on the proposal to allow detention of suspected terrorists for 90 days.
- Backbench influence may depend upon a number of factors including the size of the Government majority, party loyalty and discipline, weight of public opinion.
- Ministers expect almost as a matter of course to have to bargain and persuade if they are to limit backbench revolts.
- Ban on Foxhunting on the Statute Book because Labour MPs refused to let it go – rejecting all Government offers of compromise.
- There was extensive consultation on the Welfare Bill (2006). Ministers wrote personally to the 100 MPs with the highest concentration of IB claimants, offering to discuss the proposals with both MPs and their constituents in the MPs constituencies. Original proposals were watered down.
- Claim that Tony Blair's first defeat (Terrorism Bill in November 2005) was brought about by a failure to listen to backbenchers.
- The January 2006 defeat (Racial and Religious Hatred Bill) caused by the whips getting the numbers wrong – allowing too many Labour MPs to be absent for campaigning in a by-election. The Prime Minister was allowed to leave the Commons before the second (lost by just one vote) division.
- Backbenchers secured complete smoking ban in England in preference to the partial ban favoured (in line with Labour's 2005 Manifesto promise) by the Government.
- Education and Inspections Bill (2006), a key plank in the Labour Government's legislative programme only passed as a result of opposition support.

- View that backbenchers secured a compensation package for those most affected by the abolition of the 10p income tax rate (2008) denied by Gordon Brown, claiming he was not "pushed about" by Labour MPs.
- The 103 back-bench rebellions (30% of all divisions) during the 2007 – 08 Westminster session was the most inflicted on any governing party for more than 30 years (but 3/4 of the revolts consisted of fewer than ten Labour MP's.)
- Despite the rebellions the Government won every whipped vote.
- Other relevant points.

Study Theme 1C – Political Parties and their Policies (including the Scottish Dimension)

Question A3

"Pass" and better answers should feature developed, exemplified knowledge and understanding of:
Ideological differences within the main political parties.
Ideological differences between the main political parties.
And
Balanced comment on/analysis of the extent to which there are ideological differences within and between the main political parties.

Answers may refer to:
- British politics looks like it is becoming an increasingly ideology-free zone.
- Blair claimed he was "beyond ideology" and Cameron has said he does not do "isms".
- UK political party ideologies less clear-cut than in the past. Core ideology has largely been abandoned in favour of pragmatic policies.
- Parties moving towards the centre ground with so-called 'big-tent' policies.
- Politics is no longer a case of "one party that solely believes in a modern market economy and doesn't understand society and the other party that is solely committed to some sense of social obligation to others and doesn't understand a market economy".
- Parties fighting their political battles away from the ideological centre ground and the mainstream issues get punished; 'what works is what counts'.
- View that UK politics is characterised not by ideological differences but by who can bring about the best competitive economy, social justice and community.
- Whilst politicians on both sides like to present themselves as un-ideological, their ideologies are just becoming increasingly similar.

The Labour Party

- The 'third way' – an effort to merge some of Labour's embedded ideals with the changes made under years of Conservative government (through 'triangulation') became the unofficial ideology of the Labour Party.
- Left wing members claim that the party has abandoned its socialist roots and become 'Thatcherism with a human face'. They argue that collective action is vital in a world where individuals feel more powerless than ever before, and criticise Conservative policies (where they grudgingly acknowledge them) as being based on hostility to collective action, especially through the state.
- Resurfacing of the radical left at the 2008 party conference as a consequence of the need for a 'state' response to financial meltdown and a 'party' response to quash any possibility of a Conservative Party electoral success.
- Scottish Labour Party has not fully embraced the 'third way'.

The Conservative Party

- Cameron's third way version attempts to reconcile core Conservative principles to the changes made by years of Labour government and:
  - endorses Labour's view that poverty in Britain is a pressing issue. However his team attack measures that increase voters' reliance on the state.
  - refutes Thatcherism's claim that tax cuts are the allies of a stable economy. (New Labour cultivated the view that tax cuts would destabilise the economy.)
  - concedes that offenders sometimes merit sympathy as well as punishment thus provoking the tabloid 'hug a hoodie' jibe.
  - agrees that rights need formal, legislative protection.
  - urges party members to be less vocal in their Euroscepticism.
  - tones down the party's view on immigration claiming that Labours 'lax' immigration policies have encouraged a 'new slave trade'.
  - embraces environmental politics.
  - makes the Conservative party look more inclusive – recognition of gay and lesbian couples who cement their relationships via the new Civil Partnerships Act + promise that they too would benefit from a restored marriage tax allowance.
- Cameron's *Built to Last* (2006) endorsed by barely 1/5 in an all-party ballot. It listed 8 'values'; in a March 2006 Populus poll for The Times, respondents wrongly attributed 5 of the statements to Labour rather than the Conservatives.
- Internal differences over grammar school-social mobility, and Europe.
- Many members alienated by refusal to promise tax cuts.
- Graham Brady resigned from the front bench over betrayal of grammar schools.
- In recent leadership contests, Conservative leftists argued for greater social tolerance in order to make the party more attractive to minority groups while those on the right argued that social freedom had already gone too far and it was time for a reassertion of traditional values.
- View that the New Tories are a decaffeinated blend of New Labour.

The Liberal Democrat Party

- The belief in the rational individual is the hallmark of liberal ideology.
- Authors of *The Orange Book, Reclaiming Liberalism* (2004) showed they were keen to embrace the 'Thatcherite' economic ideas.
- Drifting into the middle ground. Plans to cut income tax and embrace market reforms in the NHS.
- View that the Liberal Democrat commitment to social justice weakening.
- Divided between modernisers, keen to bring fresh rigour to policy-making and more left-wing traditionalists.
- In rejecting either Simon Hughes or Chris Huhne as their new leader it seems to have opted against a decisive move either to the left or the right.

The Scottish Nationalist Party

- Describes itself as a democratic left-of-centre party committed to independence for Scotland, internationalist in outlook and liberal in its social policies.
- Historically collectivist (although possibility of 'mutualisation' being included in the party's manifesto for the 2011 Holyrood elections) – its main issue is between 'gradualism' and 'fundamentalism'.
- Other relevant points.

Study Theme 1D – Electoral Systems, Voting and Political Attitudes

Question A4

"Pass" and better answers should feature developed, exemplified knowledge and understanding of:
The influence of media on voting behaviour.
Other factors that influence voting behaviour.
And
Balanced comment on/analysis of the view that the media is the most important influence on voting behaviour.

Answers may refer to:
- Most people get their political news from television, which by law must remain neutral, although political parties would complain that it does not.
- Parties feel that Party Political Broadcasts are important but most people claim to either turn off or turn over.
- Around half of the UK households take a newspaper on a daily basis. Newspapers clearly biased.
- Evidence suggests that voters tend to choose a newspaper that supports their political outlook or they mainly read stories that agree with their politics.
- Many readers are neither affected by political bias nor aware of the political stance taken by their reading material.
- Political parties still court partisan press support. The *Sun* claims to have helped Labour win the last three elections.
- Newspapers court the social class, age, gender and race of their readers by building their 'political' message around what they believe their readers want to read.
- In 2005, 5 of the 10 national daily newspapers with almost 16m readers supported Labour against 3 with 10m readers who backed the Conservatives. Sunday papers split 4/4. The *News of the World*, *Sunday Mirror*, the *People* and the *Observer* with 9.4 million readers backed Labour, while, the *Sunday Times* and *Sunday Express* returned to the Conservatives, joining the *Mail on Sunday* and *Sunday Telegraph*, together with a total readership of 7 million.
- Several papers supported tactical voting; according to MORI the election coverage by the two newspapers most anguished about Iraq (*Guardian* & *Independent*) persuaded many of their readers into a tactical vote for the Liberal Democrats.
- With tabloid sales falling year-by-year many editors believe that a political front page is nigh on commercial suicide. During April 2005 more than 3/4 tabloid front pages featured stories other than the election.
- In the 2005 election, newspapers' online editions played a significant role in election coverage and were used by considerable numbers of voters, particularly the young.
- Scottish 2007 campaign fought by the media on the front pages and high in the bulletins unlike 1999 and 2003 when war reporting filled much available space. SNP sought to dampen pro Labour bias by sending poll evidence to newspaper editors to stress how many of their readers were pro-Nationalist.
- As Labour's campaign failed to impact on the SNP's poll lead, several editors turned up the heat on the Nationalists (The Sun, depicting an SNP victory with a hangman's noose).
- The final Sunday of campaigning saw four newspapers back Alex Salmond as First Minister and the Scotsman followed suit.
- Many radio listeners already have a committed political allegiance.
- Each of the parties had a website and the 2005 election was the first to feature candidate blogs with 'proxy blogs' being written for candidates whether they liked it or not.
- Lynne Featherstone who won Hornsey and Wood Green for the Liberal Democrats on a 15% swing wrote a daily blog. She felt that because journalists read it and commented on what she posted, the site 'had a significant role in raising her profile'.
- View that it is probably the day-to-day spin in the mass-market tabloids that sways some voters, particularly those least interested in politics.
- Much of the media portrayal of politicians and government is negative; impact on voter turnout?
- View that 'rational choice model' (policies, competence and leadership) has taken over from 'social structures model' (class, age, gender) as most important influence on voting behaviour.
- Party dealignment.
- Party strategists convinced that women hold the key to who wins and who loses elections.
- Constituency campaigning used to be widely viewed as a traditional, familiar but ultimately pointless activity. Recent research has shown that the more intense the local campaign the greater the turnout in that constituency. In most cases it has been found that the stronger a party's campaign is in a constituency, the better it does there in the election.
- Other relevant points.

Section B – Social Issues in the United Kingdom

Study Theme 2 – Wealth and Health Inequalities in the United Kingdom

Question B5

"Pass" and better answers should feature developed, exemplified knowledge and understanding of:
The impact of income on health.
Other factors that impact on health.
And
Balanced comment on/analysis of the impact of income on health.

Answers may refer to:
- Statistical evidence from both government-generated reports and independent health research identifies the link between income, morbidity and mortality.
- Adults in the poorest fifth twice as likely to be at risk of developing a mental illness as those on average incomes.
- Among those aged 45 to 64, 45% of men and 40% of women in the poorest fifth report a limiting longstanding illness or disability, compared with 10% and 15% respectively for those in the richest fifth.
- The rate of infant death among social classes 1 to 4 is around 4 per 1,000 live births, compared with 5.5 for those in social classes 5 to 8.
- Those at the lowest end of the social spectrum have the highest consumption of 'junk food' and lowest of fruit and vegetables.
- People on low incomes cannot afford, and seldom have access to, shops selling good food.
- Women on below average incomes are twice as likely to be obese as women on above-average earnings.
- Unskilled men have a shorter life expectancy overall.
- Better off can afford better diets, leisure activities that promote good health, better housing and safer environments.
- Middle and professional classes more likely to consult health professionals, know how to get the best out of the system, and follow positive health promotion advice.
- Better off can afford the option of private health care.

- Almost half of all adults in the poorest fifth of the population have a limiting long-standing illness or disability (twice the rate for those on average incomes).
- There is a high incidence of heart disease in poorest areas of Scotland.
- Wealthiest suburb in Scotland (Bellsquarry) has life expectancy of 87.7 years while Glasgow is 54 for males – Shettleston Man as a personification of Glasgow's ills.
- A child born in Calton, in the east end of Glasgow is three times as likely to suffer heart disease and four times as likely to be hospitalised than a child in the city's prosperous suburbs.
- Difference in life expectancy between the best and worst areas in Edinburgh is 22 years (9 years in the Highlands).
- "Biology of poverty": View that extreme poverty can alter people's generic make-up making them more susceptible to diseases such as cancer; biological factors may be just as important in explaining the gap in health and lifespan amongst rich and poor as lifestyle and diet; people who are continually exposed to stress as a result of chronic social deprivation are more likely to suffer disease and cell malfunction.
- Women from ethnic minorities are twice as likely as white women to die during childbirth or soon afterwards (Maternity Alliance Report).
- Women have lower mortality but higher morbidity rates than men.
- Only 8.5% of those dying of cancer aged over 85 die in a hospice compared with 20% of all cancer deaths – illustrating inequalities in the way that care and support are made available to older people.
- Age, ethnicity, geography, lifestyle, social class, geography, the 'postcode lottery'.
- Other relevant points.

Question B6

"Pass" and better answers should feature developed, exemplified knowledge and understanding of:
Recent government policies to reduce poverty.
The consequences of these policies to reduce poverty
And
Balanced comment on/analysis of the success of government policies to reduce poverty.

Answers may refer to:
'Welfare to Work'
- 300,000 extra lone mothers have found employment – but these strategies have left behind large families or those with disabled children.
- Some five million women (20%) and four million men (18%) belong to households in poverty. This gap is half what it was in the mid-1990s. The fall reflects the decline in the poverty rates for two kinds of single adult households in which women predominate: lone parents and single pensioners.
- There are more poor adults in relative poverty since records began in 1961.
- Number of adults without children who live in poverty has changed little in a decade.

Tax credits
- Lifted lots of lone parents and families with children out of poverty.
- Things have improved in relative terms. Fewer children now live in what would have been called poverty a decade ago.
- If government had merely increased tax allowances and benefits in line with inflation since 1999 there would be 1.7m more poor children in the UK today.
- As the number of children helped by tax credits to escape poverty has increased, so too has the number needing tax credits to do so.
- Half the children in poverty are in families already doing paid work; this means that the key proposition behind the anti-poverty strategy – 'work is the route out of poverty' does not apply for many people. The underlying problem is low pay (despite **NMW**).
- Target to halve child poverty by 2010 and end it by 2020 looks 'unattainable' as it would mean 300,000 children being moved out of poverty in each of the four years to 2010-11.
- 250,000 children in Scotland live in poverty.
- Most of the young adults aged 16 to 24 now in poverty, were children when the Government first pledged to abolish child poverty in 1999. Two-thirds of them are single and without dependent children, many still living at home with their parents.
- UK child poverty is still above the EU average.

The [Means Tested] Minimum Income Guarantee and Pension Credit
- The big fall in poverty among pensioners, especially single pensioners, claimed as a major success of the anti-poverty strategy.
- These can have rapid and substantial effects on those with the lowest incomes but do not address the root of the problem.

Sure Start
- Recent research has proved it to be both popular and on track.
- Critics claim that it is ill-targeted (particularly failing ethnic minority groups), poorly implemented and a colossal waste of money.

Scottish Government initiatives
- Free school meals, reduction and phased elimination of prescription charges, the "Equally Well" agenda, A Curriculum for Excellence, 3-18 (to improve life skills and employability).

Fuel Poverty
- When more than 10% of income has to be spent on keeping warm.
- Government policy aims to eradicate fuel poverty among the elderly, disabled, children and long-term sick by 2010.
- Claim that there has been a significant reduction in the number of fuel-poor homes.
- Many households have been helped with cost of installing insulation and central heating.
- UK Government proposal (2008) that data identifying poorer families could be shared with companies to ensure they pay cheaper rates. (Most of the energy companies have "social tariffs".)
- Agreement reached with the power companies to increase the amount of money they spend in helping people get on to lower tariffs and helping people insulate their homes.
- Energywatch claims more than 4 million households in fuel poverty (2.5m officially).
- Median income rises most years, so meeting any poverty reduction target is like "running up and down an escalator" according to Beverley Hughes (Minister for Children).
- Overall improvements in health (**increased health expenditure**) or educational achievement (**"Education, Education, Education"**) have sometimes left the most disadvantaged lagging even further behind.
- Well-meaning anti-poverty measures have nurtured a "why bother" society.
- The clawing back of benefits as people find better-paying jobs has undercut incentives for people to strive to improve their lot.
- The Tax Credits 'fiasco'.

- Those moving from the minimum wage to one of two thirds of average earnings can take home as little as 11p of every extra pound they earn as a consequence of the high marginal tax rates created by the benefits system.
- A growth in means-testing or other forms of targeting has allowed limited resources to be focused on those in greatest need but may have led to problems of take up and of widening disincentives to work or save.
- Complexity of claiming means tested benefits.
- 40% of ethnic minorities live in poverty. This is double the proportion for whites. Even Indians and Chinese are much likelier than whites to be poor despite outperforming them at school.
- The 30% poverty rate amongst disabled adults aged 25 to retirement is twice the non-disabled rate AND higher than a decade ago.
- View that the UK is now a nation of greater income inequality (more people now in relative poverty than since records began in 1961), in which the plight of the very poor has worsened.
- Of 56 poverty indicators tracked by the Joseph Rowntree Foundation (2008), three quarters have stalled or are getting worse – a position being made all the more fragile with the onset of recession.
- View that government fuel poverty measures won't fix the problem – people will still be left out in the cold.
- Other relevant points.

SECTION C – INTERNATIONAL ISSUES

Study Theme 3A – The Republic of South Africa

Question C7

"Pass" and better answers should feature developed, exemplified knowledge and understanding of:
Inequalities between racial groups in South Africa.
Inequalities within racial groups in South Africa.
And
Balanced comment on/analysis of the view that inequalities exist only *between* different racial groups.

Answers may refer to:

- South Africa has one of the most unequal income distributions in the world.
- The poor (two in three blacks living below the poverty level) and unemployed remain disproportionately black.
- Unemployment rates (2007): Black 30.5%, Coloured 19.4%, Indian/Asian 9.6%, and White 4.5%.
- Except for Whites, female unemployment is substantially higher than for males.
- Whites have 9.2% of the population but 45.3% of income.
- Whites control 90% of the assets and big companies.
- Only 7% of the stock exchange (target 25%) has moved into black hands.
- 90% of commercially viable farmland remains in white hands and the land redistribution target set for 2014 seems unlikely to be met.
- By 2000, blacks held 72% of civil service jobs as a result of expensively retiring 'Apartheid bureaucrats'.
- Poor education limits the social mobility of many South Africans.
- 22% of Blacks have no schooling; for Whites the figure is 1.4%.
- 59-77% of children in the best performing state schools are white.
- University entrance qualifications are most common amongst Indians and Whites, least common amongst Coloureds and Blacks.

- Many black homes are without water (20%), and electricity (13%): the populations of the shanty towns continue to grow. (More than half of local areas do not provide sanitation, clean water or rubbish to more than 40% of their households.)
- Housing shortage in Western Cape adds to tension between Coloureds (mixed race South Africans) and Blacks.
- Black life expectancy 60 years; White life expectancy 73 years.
- Whites far more likely to have private health care.
- Judiciary remains largely white.
- View that class is replacing race as the defining social dynamic of the South African 'cappuccino society'.
- Black Economic Empowerment policies have created a new Black middle class.
- 'Black Diamonds' said to number 2.6 million (2007), – a 30% increase in less than two years, – and to account for 12% of South Africa's black adults and 28% of the country's buying power (more than half of black buying power.)
- Distribution of wealth amongst Blacks is greater than in any other racial group in South Africa.
- Dissatisfaction of poorer Blacks is mirrored by recent hostility to immigrants from Zimbabwe, Mozambique and Somali shopkeepers.
- "Poor" whites come almost entirely from the Afrikaner community who make up 60% of the white population; they claim that the government's poverty alleviation programmes ignore them.
- Statistically, unemployment amongst white South Africans has doubled since the end of apartheid, with estimates of 10% of the white population now too poor to live in traditionally white working and middle class areas and having to live in conditions previously the reserve of poor blacks.
- Other relevant points.

Study Theme 3B – The People's Republic of China

Question C8

"Pass" and better answers should feature developed, exemplified knowledge and understanding of:
Greater freedom as a result of social and economic reform.
Other factors that influence the level of demand for political reform in China
And
Balanced comment on/analysis of the view that there is little demand for political reform (in China) because of greater social and economic freedom.

Answers may refer to:

- Chinese Communist Party has been accused of trying to spend its way out of trouble so as to retain its monopoly of political power.
- Mr Hu's "Harmonious Society" is the dominant socio-economic policy.
- Social controls have loosened and unprecedented economic freedom has been allowed.
- Demise of the *danwai* and *hukou*.
- Price controls have almost gone.
- Wealth creation encouraged.
- Labour contract law of Jan 2008 made it much harder to sack underperforming workers and created a role for trade unions in discipline, safety, pay and working hours.
- Agricultural reforms have brought wealth to some farmers.
- Tax reforms and subsidies have increased rural incomes (but urban incomes have grown faster.)
- Free education for rural children – although many still have to pay for textbooks.

- Sexual harassment of women made unlawful in 2005.
- New medical insurance scheme (2003), financed by central government, set up in place of long-discarded barefoot doctor scheme.
- To ease agony of thousands who lost only child in Sichuan earthquake, doctors to provide free treatments to reverse sterilisation procedures.
- Increase in right to legal representation
- In 2006 the Supreme Court reclaimed the power to review all death sentences.
- Party membership extended to new business classes.
- 2008 decision to "transform the entire rural policy" by giving farmers the right to rent out or sell the plots they lease from local "collectives" under "household responsibility contracts".
- CCP is widely seen as holding the country together and there is competition to join it.
- Chinese people have never enjoyed such social freedom and economic prosperity (although this is unevenly distributed) and show no great dissatisfaction with the CPC.
- View that economic reform has made huge strides and it is time to turn to politics.
- CCP controlled experiments in democracy.
- Mr Wen talks of "thought liberation" and making the party more accountable.
- A publication (Storming The Fortress) originating from the Party's academy for senior officials outlines "urgent" steps for political reform including freeing up the press. In accordance with the official line that political reform is on the CPC agenda, it states that the goal of the reform of China's political institutions is to become a democratic country under the rule of law by 2020.
- Suggestion that "Civic" organisations (to party officials NGO sounds too much like organised opposition) are to be given a role in "voicing the concerns of the people."
- CCP has been accused of "populism" – trying to boost its standing amongst the downtrodden and pandering to rising nationalism (protests at what the Chinese see as unfair foreign criticism over Tibet.) In 2007 the government ran an online survey on changes to China's public holiday pattern.
- Mr Hu on record as saying that China will never copy Western style democracy as this would be a "blind alley for China".
- Demand for political reform greatest in the provinces: Tibet, Xinjiang, Guangdong, Hong Kong – but each has a different 'political' agenda.
- Urban and rural protests (contradictions within the people) have increased in recent years – mainly fuelled by official wrongdoing and corruption - but politically organised opposition is rare.
- Award of the Olympics to China encouraged a speaking out on 'sensitive' topics.
- Internet has created an opportunity for vigorous debate that hardly existed a decade ago.
- CCP intolerant of opposition and relies on the support of the armed forces (biggest annual expenditure increases tend to be on the armed forces.)
- CCP remains dictatorial and determined to crush any organised dissent.
- CCP controls the media: outspoken newspapers closed, editors sacked, journalists jailed.
- Dissidents who net post views are jailed.
- Human Rights activists and members of unauthorised religious groups continue to be harassed/jailed.
- The CCP concept of 'democracy' does not extend to allowing organised opposition. All officially sanctioned comments are careful to stress the need to maintain the CPC's monopoly on power.

- December 2008: more than 300 of China's most prominent activists issued a wide-ranging appeal for democratic reform (Charter 08). Chief organiser Liu Xiabo detained and other signatories threatened or questioned.
- As economic growth falters, and unemployment and suspicion of officialdom (the contaminated milk scandal) rises, political activism may increase.
- Other relevant points.

Study Theme 3C – The United States of America

Question C9

"Pass" and better answers should feature developed, exemplified knowledge and understanding of:
The achievement of the American Dream by ethnic minorities.
The non-achievement of the American Dream by ethnic minorities.
And
Balanced comment on/analysis of the extent to which ethnic minorities achieve the American Dream.

Answers may refer to:

The *American Dream* as having the freedom that allows all citizens to achieve their goals in life through hard work; for many it is the opportunity to have financial security, a home, successful career and the ability to send their children to the best schools possible.

Achievement
- Growing black well-educated, well-paid, home-owning, middle class.
- There are many successful Hispanic entrepreneurs, particularly those of Cuban origin.
- Asians build on their educational success to become high earners (especially those of Chinese, Japanese and Korean origin.)
- A number of Native American tribes (California's Cabazons and New Mexico's Sandias) have benefited from the gaming (casino) industry. Others (Arizona's Navajos) from their control of natural resources.
- Enhanced by a number of high profile appointed & elected ethnic minority political figures. "Disproportionate" representation is due to a number of factors.
- The 2008 election of Barack Obama as president.

Non-Achievement
- Blacks experience twice the average unemployment rate, earn 35% less on average than whites, have lower home ownership rates (48%), are more likely to underachieve in education, to live in crime ridden, almost jobless ghettos and have poorer health and less access to health care.
- 69% of blacks born out of wedlock and 70% of these births are to single (not cohabiting) mothers.
- Only 5% of firms are black-owned, though blacks account for 13% of America's population.
- Hispanics endure high poverty rates, similar home ownership rates to blacks, slightly lower unemployment rates but a slightly higher average income than blacks, lower educational attainment levels than both blacks and whites, and restricted access to health care.
- 50% of all Hispanic children in America born out of wedlock with more than half of young Hispanic children in families headed by a single mother living below the federal poverty line, compared with 21% raised by a married couple.
- Native American reservations have some of the highest rates of poverty (almost one in three), unemployment, welfare dependency, school dropout, alcoholism, and other indicators of poverty and social distress (life expectancy for Native Americans in Arizona is 54.7 years) of any communities in the United States.

- 38% of families headed by a Native American single mother live in poverty.
- Part played by Affirmative Action and racial preferences (each of which incur both white and black opposition) in helping blacks achieve the American Dream.
- Julian Bond of the NAACP claims that racism (Jan 6, 2007) is still "epidemic" in America. Black conservatives, while never denying that racism persists, think it is much less severe than before and no longer the main obstacle to black advancement.
- Black students who study hard are accused of "acting white" and are ostracised by their peers.
- Until the Clinton reforms of the 1990s, welfare often paid better than an entry-level job and the counter-culture taught young blacks that working for "chump change" was beneath their dignity.
- Even when blacks earn as much as whites, the whites are typically far wealthier, blacks save, whites invest.
- The sub-prime mortgage crisis likely to cost many blacks their homes.
- Blacks are more likely to be jailed but they do commit more crimes – the black murder rate (2005) was seven times higher than that for whites and Hispanics combined.
- Other relevant points.

Study Theme 3D – The European Union

Question C10

"Pass" and better answers should feature developed, exemplified knowledge and understanding of:
The decision making powers of the Council of Ministers.
The decision making powers of other EU institutions.
And
Balanced comment on/analysis of the view that Council of Ministers is the most important decision making institution in the EU.

Answers may refer to:

The Council of Ministers
- Is the main law-and-budget making body, which brings together national ministers (of, for example, finance, foreign affairs or agriculture).
- Often makes decisions by qualified majority, a weighted system of national votes, but on some issues (taxation) it has to be unanimous.
- Co-ordinates the broad economic policies of the member states.
- Concludes, on behalf of the Union, international agreements between the EU and one or more states or international organisations.
- May issue regulations, directives, decisions, common actions or common positions, recommendations or opinions.
- Can adopt conclusions, declarations or resolutions.
- Defines and implements the European Union's common foreign policy, based on guidelines set by **The European Council** which is made up of the 27 heads of government and meets four times a year, nominates the commission president and defines the general political guidelines of the European Union.

The European Commission has the sole right of initiating legislation, administers the budget and has other independent powers including deciding competition cases and representing the Union in trade negotiations.
- Is the origin of 80% of laws passed at national level.
- Answers to national governments – through the council – and to parliament.
- In principle, makes legislative proposals but these are examined within the Council, which can make modifications before adopting them.

The European Parliament (785 directly elected members) is an active participant in the legislative process.
- May adopt legislation jointly with the Council using the co-decision procedure but has no say in some matters such as justice and home affairs.
- Approves the choice of Commission president and can dismiss the entire Commission, but not individual Commissioners
- Shares with the Council authority over the EU budget and can therefore influence EU spending. At the end of the procedure, it adopts or rejects the budget in its entirety.

The European Court of Justice acts as the European Union's highest legal authority in areas for which the Union is responsible.

The Court of Auditors checks EU spending and qualifies the accounts every year.
- Other relevant points.

Study Theme 3E – The Politics of Development in Africa

Question C11

"Pass" and better answers should feature developed, exemplified knowledge and understanding of:
The influence of NGOs on development.
Other factors that influence development.
And
Balanced comment on/analysis of the influence of NGOs on development.

Answers may refer to:

NGOs
- Work closely with many UN programmes and agencies.
- Respond to "development threatening" emergency and crisis situations.
- Good at small projects; handle these well and are sensitive to the needs of the local population, involving it in the decision making process; promote bottom-up development.
- Emphasise the "African" delivery of development.
- Create the physical human and social capital that raises the likelihood of future social and economic development.
- Neither create dependency nor discourage local enterprise.
- Contribute to the international debate on development.
- May be used for political ends by governments that source them.
- May make things worse by easing the pressure for reform.
- May prevent an immediate famine but undercut local farmers, thus risking future famine.
- Eventually leave it to local government structures to sustain any improvements.
- Accused of a lack of transparency and accountability, of duplication of effort, and of embarking on short-term impact projects.
- Seen by their fiercest critics as a new form of colonialism.
- Increasingly asked by donors to provide measurable proof that they make a difference.
- View that aid is fragmenting: there are too many agencies financing too many small projects, using too many different procedures. "Fragmentation is the opposite of effectiveness" (Lennart Bage, head of IFAD).
- Operate at the whim of the government in whose country they are working.
- Claim by Professor Sir David King (former UK Government Chief Scientific Advisor) that NGOs from Europe and America are turning African countries against sophisticated farming methods including GM crops in favour of indigenous and organic approaches that cannot deliver the continent's much needed "green revolution".

Other Influences
- The attitude of African governments – some welcome NGO activity, particularly in education and healthcare provision, but others see them as interfering or even as a threat.
- 'Good governance'.
- Debt.
- Globalisation.
- Commodity prices, food prices, and the terms of trade.
- Bilateral and multi-lateral aid agreements.
- Conflict; countries affected by civil violence may lose, on average, just over two percentage points of growth a year and need 14 years to get back to normal.
- Investment in infrastructure.
- Land ownership.
- Population growth.
- Natural disasters.
- Other relevant points.

Study Theme 3F – Global Security

Question C12

"Pass" and better answers should feature developed, exemplified knowledge and understanding of:
The ways in which United Nations may respond to threats to international peace and security.
The consequences of United Nations responses to selected threats to international peace and security.
And
Balanced comment on/analysis of the effectiveness of the United Nations in dealing with threats to international peace and global security.

Answers may refer to:
- The UN Charter requires that all members agree to accept and carry out the decisions of the Security Council.
- The UN Charter entitles the Security Council to take action in cases of a "threat to peace, breach of the peace or act of aggression." However "nothing should authorise intervention in matters essentially within the domestic jurisdiction of any state."
- Security Council may investigate disputes, recommend a political solution to a dispute, oversee cease-fires, patrol disputed borders, instruct UN members to impose sanctions to either prevent or stop aggression, to assist in taking military action against an aggressor.
- Security Council has five permanent members (p5) and 10 non-permanent members.
- Each Council member has one vote with decisions on procedural matters requiring support from at least 9/15 members and those on substantive matters the support of 9 members, including each of the p5.
- Some see this veto as a safety valve and consider that it is much better to have an obstructionist member on board than a furious one walking out.
- Inability of the p5 to agree on what should be done has often slowed the deployment of peacekeepers where they are most needed, (Darfur) and has not stopped the nuclear posturing of Iran and North Korea (Russia and China watered down the text of resolutions and sanctions proposals).
- UN ignored by USA over Iraq (The Bush doctrine).
- View that regional organisations are often better placed/equipped to deal with threats to international peace and security.
- The explosion of civil wars, ethnic and religious violence at the end of the Cold War caught the UN by surprise. It had no standing army, no effective military staff, and very little peacekeeping experience. Mistakes were made – slaughter in Rwanda and the Srebrenica massacre.
- Human Security Report 2005 (OUP) documented a 40% decrease in violent conflict, an 80% decrease in the "most deadly" conflicts and an 80% decrease in genocide since the end of the Cold War – largely attributed to UN efforts.
- There has been a six-fold increase in the number of soldiers and military observers deployed world wide between 1998-2007. UN peacekeeping forces often under-strength, under-resourced and under-equipped. (Powerful countries decide on the missions (and pay for them) while poorer countries supply the soldiers.)
- The UN has been credited with helping reduce the number of conflicts between states, as well as calming civil wars from Bosnia to Haiti, from Cambodia to Sudan, from Congo to Lebanon.
- Importance of the Peacebuilding Commission – finances reconstruction in countries emerging from conflict (Congo, southern Sudan, Liberia, Lebanon, Cote d'Ivoire).
- Concerns over the effectiveness of the UN have led to calls for the reform of the institution balanced by the view that ultimately it is member states that must take action and therefore bear the responsibility.
- UN Charter does not spell out what counts as "the use of force" in cyberspace (alleged Russian cyber attacks on Estonia, in 2007, and Georgia in 2008).
- Other relevant points.

MODERN STUDIES HIGHER
PAPER 2
2009

Question 1

Avril Beattie (Source A) claims: "The percentage of women in senior positions in the public services is well below that of men, so it comes as no surprise that the UK has the largest gender pay gap in the European Union".

Source C1 (a) shows that the percentage of women in senior management in the public services *is* well below that of men.

However Source C1 (b) shows that the UK *does not* have the largest gender pay gap in the EU. Cyprus and Germany each have a larger gender pay gap than the UK.

QUESTION 2

(a) Avril Beattie (Source A) claims: "Well over half of women say that having children is the biggest obstacle they face in pursuing a successful career".
Source C2 (a) shows only 48% of women claim this to be so.

(b) Jim Waugh (Source B) claims: "More girls than boys are going into both full time higher/further education and employment". Source C2 shows that more girls than boys *are* going into full time higher/further education.
However more boys than girls are going into employment after leaving school.

QUESTION 3

Jim Waugh (Source B) claims: "the UK has one of the highest percentages of women in senior management in the world". Source C3 shows that the UK *does not* have one of the highest percentages of women in senior management posts in the world. The majority of countries featured in the table have a higher percentage.

QUESTION 4

Credit will be given for
A style appropriate to a report (sub-headings, chapters etc) with:
- an introduction that indicates an awareness of the role to be adopted and makes a clear recommendation
- developed arguments in support of the recommendation
- identification of and comment on (rebuttal of) counter arguments
- synthesis of source information
- provision and use of appropriate background knowledge
- an overall conclusion.

Argument for the proposal could include:
- continued existence of pay gap
- low female representation in senior management positions in the public services
- gender career stereotyping
- the glass ceiling
- slow pace of progress towards gender equality
- other relevant points featured in the source material.

Argument against the proposal could include:
- importance of meritocracy
- more girls now going into further/higher education
- proposal is "patronising"
- loss of talented males to the private sector
- there are more deserving causes than the improvement of opportunities for the already well-paid
- other relevant points featured in the source material.

Credit knowledge-based argument developed from references in:

Source A
- The glass ceiling
- The gender pay gap and Examples of unequal pay to be found in the UK
- The Women and Work Commission (report into closing the gender pay gap)
- "Five C's" (cleaning, catering, caring, clerical, cashiering)

Source B
- *There has been a great deal of gender equality legislation in recent years* Employment Equality (Sex Discrimination) Regulations 2005; Work and Families Act, 2006; Gender Equality Duty 2006; Sex Discrimination (Amendment) Regulations 2008)
- *In addition, diversity targets have been set for the Civil Service* (30% of top management posts to be held by women by April 2008 and new 10 point plan issued in July 2008)
- *We have reached a point where equality laws are actually holding back women's careers.* In July 2008, Nicola Brewer, chief executive of the Equalities and Human Rights Commission claimed that calls to the Commission's helpline from women who had lost their jobs after becoming pregnant suggested that they were paying a heavy price for their new rights. She said that her fears had deepened earlier in the year when Sir Alan Sugar was quoted as saying "If someone comes into an interview and you think to yourself there is a possibility that this woman might have a child and therefore take time off, it is a bit of a psychological negative thought"
- *UK's many social problems*
- *A healthy work – life balance.* Findings of the British Household Panel Survey: women may be redefining themselves as mothers who work rather than career women who happen to have children. The Survey which involved 3,800 couples over eight years, found that women with part-time jobs reported greater job satisfaction than those in full-time work.

Source C
Credit development and comment on any of the statistical sources: the UK pay gap *is* above the European average. The UK has a large gap because lots of women work. In other EU countries only the higher skilled (and thus better paid) can find jobs.

Other background knowledge-based argument may include reference to:

- The 2008 Sex and Power Report (revealed the continued existence of glass ceilings across a range of professions)
- Equality Bill 2008-2009
- Equal pay claims in which Scottish local authorities have had to increase the pay of female staff to that of men in 'comparable' posts and award back-dated settlements
- On-going individualist v collectivist debate
- Other relevant points.

MODERN STUDIES HIGHER
PAPER 1
2010

Section A – Political Issues in the United Kingdom

Study Theme 1A – Devolved Decision Making in Scotland

Question A1

"Pass" and better answers should feature developed, exemplified knowledge and understanding of:

The part played by Scottish representatives at Westminster
The debate surrounding Scotland's future with regard to the union
And
Balanced comment/analysis on whether Scottish representation is needed at Westminster.

Answers may refer to:
- The role of Scotland's 59 MPs, the Scottish Office (part of the Ministry for Justice) and the Secretary of State for Scotland (2009 Jim Murphy) in representing Scotland's interests at Westminster.
- The devolved (health, education, transport, etc.) and reserved (constitutional matters, social security, foreign policy, etc.) powers. Most legislation affecting Scotland is passed in the Scottish Parliament although the UK Parliament at Westminster remains sovereign.
- The number of Scottish-based MPs in the 2009 UK Cabinet (18%) inc. Prime Minister Gordon Brown and Chancellor of the Exchequer Alistair Darling.
- Criticism of rising cost of Scotland Office and there have been calls to scrap post of Secretary of State for Scotland. First meeting of Secretary of State for Scotland and SNP Ministers in June 2009.
- Legislation including phased abolition of prescription charges, freezing of Council Tax, abolition of graduate endowment fee, ban on smoking in enclosed public places, etc.
- The calls for increased powers for the Scottish Parliament including greater fiscal independence, control over nuclear power and weapons based in Scotland, control of elections, fishing industry, etc. Renaming of Scottish Executive as the Scottish Government.
- The West Lothian Question and responses. The Conservatives Democracy Task Force argued for English MP only votes on English only laws but incorporating English-only Committee and Report stages but a vote of all MPs at Second and Third Readings. Cameron has talked of an 'English grand committee'.
- The SNP's 'National Conversation' and proposal for a referendum on Scotland's constitutional future and the pro-union parties Scottish Constitutional Commission (led by Sir Kenneth Calman) which was tasked to review devolution (but not independence). Calman's proposals for greater fiscal powers and control over speed limits, drink driving laws and elections in Scotland.
- The on-going debate over the Barnett Formula and/or the future effects of Barnett.
- Increased use of Legislative Consent Motions (formerly Sewell Motions).
- Recent calls for greater devolution of power following MPs expenses scandal.
- Other relevant points.

Study Theme 1B - Decision Making in Central Government

Question A2

"Pass" and better answers should feature developed, exemplified knowledge and understanding of:

Opportunities for Parliament (HoC) and (HoL) to control the Executive
Extent to which Parliament has been able to control the Executive
And
Balanced comment/analysis on the view that Parliament has little control over the Executive.

Answers may refer to:
- For full marks an answer should make reference to the House of Lords.
- Parliament has two functions: one legislative the other to scrutinise the work of the Executive. There is a view that Parliament has become less effective in holding the Executive to account in recent years.
- Debates in the House of Commons Chamber (and Westminster Hall) including those held within the legislative process (eg Second Reading, Report Stage and Third Reading). Debates also take place during the Committee stage of bills (usually in General Committees rather than in House of Commons). Also, Adjournment Debate – half hour at the end of the day's business and Opposition Days (around 20 days) when opposition parties set agenda.
- House of Lords debates include those also within legislative process and general debates that are held on Thursdays. There are also many short debates of up to 90 minutes on days when legislation is being considered or at the end of the day's business.
- Votes in HoC. Government defeated over plan to restrict rights of Ghurkas to settle in UK (04/09) and plan to hold votes across England (06/09). Government forced to bring compensation package after abolition of 10p tax rate.
- Votes in the HoL. Government defeated in Nov. 2008 over issue of keeping people's DNA and fingerprints on the police national database; in Oct. 2008 over extension to length of time terrorist suspect could be held without charge (from 28 to 42 days) and in June '09 over donations to political parties from tax exiles.
- Parliament Acts state that HoL cannot delay (in view of Speaker) money bills (taxes/public spending) for more than one month or public bills for more than two parliamentary sessions or one calendar year. These provisions only apply to bills that originate in the House of Commons.
- 'Sailsbury Convention' where Lords does not oppose legislation proposed in Government's election manifesto.
- Work of Select Committees which examine the work of the main government departments in terms of expenditure, administration and policy and Public bill committees (formerly standing committees) which examine legislation.
- Question Time – Begins business of Commons four times per week. PMQT is on Wednesday's for 30 minutes.
- Size of Government majority. Can work two ways: small majority may help to maintain party discipline whereas large majority may encourage rebellions eg over part privatisation of Royal Mail (plans later shelved).
- Use of the Whip.
- Calls for widespread reform of Parliament inc. reduction in Executive power after recent expenses/cash for amendments scandals.
- Rare threat of vote of no confidence.
- Other relevant points.

Study Theme 1C - Political Parties and their Policies (including the Scottish Dimension)

Question A3

"Pass" and better answers should feature developed, exemplified knowledge and understanding of:

Ways in which different political parties decide policy
Extent of influence of party members in deciding policy in different parties

And

Balanced comment/analysis of the extent to which party members decide their party's policies.

Answers may refer to:
- For full marks answers must refer to more than one political party.

Conservative Party/Scottish Conservative Party
- Traditionally policy making decided by leadership but reformed under Hague.
- National Conservative Convention and Conservative Political Forum allow party members to have input into policy but they remain advisory. Cameron has indicated that he is in support of the ideas, more policy to be decided by party members locally. Challenge Groups and Taskforces set up to allow party members opportunity to contribute.
- Direct ballots of party membership on selected issues but issues closely controlled by leadership as individual members cannot initiate own proposals or ballots.

Labour Party/Scottish Labour Party
- Labour Party consists of Constituency Labour Parties, affiliated trade unions, socialist societies and the Co-operative Party with which it has an electoral agreement. Members who are elected to parliamentary positions take part in the Parliamentary Labour Party (PLP).
- Party's decision-making bodies at a national level formally include the National Executive Committee (NEC), Labour Party Conference and National Policy Forum (NPF) although in practice the parliamentary leadership has the final say on policy.
- The Labour Party Constitution states that Party policies making up the Labour Party programme should be approved by the Conference, subject to receiving two thirds support. The election manifesto, which consists of policies from the programme, has to be agreed between the parliamentary leadership and the NEC.
- Leadership/NEC proposes programme and conference votes to support/reject programme with CLPs, affiliated organisations and trade unions having weighting according to number of members.
- Policy in the Labour Party is made through a process called Partnership in Power (PiP) which is designed to involve all party stakeholders (inc. ordinary party members). PiP does this through a rolling programme of policy development and a year-round dialogue between the party and government. Development of policy is carried out by six policy commissions.

Liberal Democrats/Scottish Liberal Democrats
- Policy making body is the Federal Conference. Twice a year, in spring and autumn, elected representatives from the Liberal Democrat constituency parties assemble at the party conference to establish federal party policy. Representatives from every local party, organised around parliamentary constituencies, are elected to attend federal conference.
- Conference decides policy matters on national and 'English' issues; separate Scottish Liberal Democrat Party makes policy decisions on Scottish issues.
- Every two years, conference representatives elect a Federal Policy Committee (FPC) which is responsible for the production of the policy papers that are debated at Conference, and is responsible for election manifestos. Party members discuss policy papers in local and regional meetings, and their representatives then debate and vote on policy motions and papers at Conference. Conference also debates motions submitted by local parties and conference representatives.

Scottish National Party
- Members can submit motions on policy and national strategy to be discussed by the party at national level.
- Local branches are drawn together to form a Constituency Association. Branches and CAs send representatives to the two national bodies that agree the policies of the Party – The National Council and Annual National Conference. Annual Conference is the supreme governing body of the Party and elects the National Executive Committee, the leadership of the Party, which deals with the day-to-day running of its affairs.
- Credit candidates who make comparisons between parties as to the extent to which party members decide policies.
- Credit candidates who appreciate decision making structures within parties change when in office.
- Other relevant points.

Study Theme 1D – Electoral Systems, Voting and Political Attitudes

Question A4

"Pass" and better answers should feature developed, exemplified knowledge and understanding of:

The main features of the STV and FPTP electoral systems
The effect of the STV and the FPTP electoral systems on the way that voters are represented

And

Balanced comment/analysis of whether STV provides for better representation than FPTP.

Answers may refer to:
STV
- First used in Scotland for Scottish local government elections of May 2007.
- Large multi-member constituencies.
- Voters list candidates in order of preference within, as well as between, parties.
- To gain election, candidates are required to gain a pre-determined quota of votes. Where this does not happen, the second, third, etc, preference of voters is used until all the representatives are elected.

FPTP
- Used for UK Parliament elections.
- Simple majority system.
- Candidate with most votes wins; party with most MPs forms the government.
- STV is a system of proportional representation (PR) so notionally fairer.
- Claim that few votes are 'wasted' under STV and that almost every voter gets at least partial representation.
- No need for tactical voting.
- Voters can choose between candidates both within and between parties; can express preferences between the abilities/attributes of individual candidates.
- Scottish local election results of 2007 saw only two councils have single-party administrations, Glasgow and North Lanarkshire. Labour's majority on Glasgow City Council fell from 64 to 11.

- Most local government administrations are made up of coalitions (21 of 32 Scottish councils have more than one party in the administration). As a result there has been an increase in 'compromise politics' which is not necessarily better representation.
- STV gives more opportunity for voters to choose female or minority ethnic candidates but local political parties continue to decide who stands for their party.
- STV breaks the direct link between voters and individual representative but it is argued that accountability has increased, and through this better representation, as there is no such thing as a safe seat. The Electoral Reform Society Scotland argues that councillors are more visible, more approachable and working harder as a consequence of STV's introduction.
- Recent debate over PR for Westminster.
- FPTP retains close representative-constituency link and usually produces majority government.
- Other relevant points.

Section B – Social Issues in the United Kingdom

Study Theme 2 – Wealth and Health Inequalities in the United Kingdom

Question B5

"Pass" and better answers should feature developed, exemplified knowledge and understanding of:

Lifestyle choices and their effect on health
Other factors which impact on health

And

Balanced comment/analysis on the impact of lifestyle choices on health.

Answers may refer to:
- Evidence of health inequalities expressed in terms of life expectancy, mortality and morbidity rates, etc.
- Evidence may be drawn from wide range of reports eg 'Equally Well: Report of Ministerial Task Force 2008' or 'Inequalities in Health 1981-2001' published in 2007, Scottish Household Survey, etc.
- Lifestyle choices: smoking, alcohol consumption, diet, use of illegal drugs, extent of exercise, uptake of preventative care services, etc., are factors that impact on health.
- Poorest groups/people in poorest areas make worst life style choices ie smoke more and have higher alcohol consumption; more likely to use illegal drugs; take less exercise; have poorer diets and make less use of preventative health care.
- Other factors that affect good health:
  - Local environment – quality of housing, community facilities, extent of crime, etc.
  - Individual circumstances – income levels, unemployment, single parent, carer, age, etc.
  - Gender.
  - Type/nature of employment – professional, labourer, stress of work, etc.
  - Quality of, and access to, local health care services.
  - Hereditary/biological factors.
- Even allowing for individual lifestyle choices, poorest groups still far more likely to die younger (between eight and ten years) and experience poorer health than those in wealthiest groups. Countries with lower income inequalities have a lower health gap.
- Other relevant points.

Question B6

"Pass" and better answers should feature developed, exemplified knowledge and understanding of:
- Government policies to reduce gender and/or ethnic inequalities
- Impact of government policies

And

Balanced comment on/analysis of the extent to which government policies have reduced gender and/or ethnic inequalities.

Answers may refer to:
- Equal Pay Act (1970); Sex Discrimination Act (1975) and Sex Discrimination Regulations (2008); Equality Act (2006); The Commission for Equality and Human Rights (2007); Gender Equality Duty Code of Practice (2007) places legal responsibility on public authorities to demonstrate that they treat men and women fairly; Women's Enterprise Task Force (2006); Equality Bill 2008 includes provision that forces companies to publish pay rates.
- Work and Families Act (2006) extended the right to request flexible working; extended further 2009.
- CTC and Working Tax Credit. Government sees affordable childcare ('wraparound childcare') as crucial to narrowing the wage gap.
- Minimum Wage has disproportionately benefited women and minorities. Maternity and paternity leave.
- Skills Strategy (2003) to address the fact that over 50% of women in part time work are working below their skill level.
- Race Relations Acts; Race Relations (Amendment) Act, 2000.
- Ethnic Minority Employment Task Force (2004) to tackle unemployment among black and Asian people.
- One Scotland.
- Women now make up 60% of the university population; success of women in reaching senior posts varies from place to place. Glass ceiling only cracked, not broken. Women make up 46% of all millionaires and are expected to own 60% of the UK's wealth by 2010.
- Women make up only 19.3% of MPs, less than 10% of the senior judiciary, national newspaper editors and senior police officers; only 11% of directors in FTSE 100 firms are women despite accounting for over half of the UK population and 46% of the labour force.
- Sex and Power Report 2007.
- Gender pay gap: UK women in full time work earn 12.8% less per hour than men (2009). Gender pay gap has widened in some cases in recent years. Pay gap higher in the private sector than in the public sector. Higher women rise up the pay ladder, the greater pay gap becomes.
- Occupational segregation.
- In 2008 National Audit Office found the employment rate for ethnic minority population was 60% compared to 74% in general population. This gap had narrowed by only 1.3% in 20 years.
- Growing evidence of a 'race pay gap' which sees black and Asian workers earn up to 15% less than white counter parts.
- Only 4.3% of board members are from ethnic minority groups despite accounting for 8.5% of workforce ('Race for Opportunity').
- Women from Black Caribbean, Pakistani and Bangladeshi groups most likely to face a higher risk of unemployment, lower pay and have fewer prospects for promotion. EOC's 'Moving on up?' report 2007.
- References to health policies and success or otherwise in reducing gender and race inequalities will be credited.
- Other relevant points.

Section C – International Issues

Study Theme 3A – The Republic of South Africa

Question C7

"Pass" and better answers should feature developed, exemplified knowledge and understanding of:

Main features of South African political system
Extent to which different parties are represented in South African politics
And
Balanced comment/analysis on the extent to which South Africa is a multi-party democracy.

Answers may refer to:
- South Africa is a constitutional democracy with a three-tier system of government.
- Federal state with nine provincial governments; each province elects a provincial legislature consisting of between 30 and 80 members. These legislatures have the power to raise provincial taxes and make laws.
- Bicameral parliament elected every five years, comprising the 400 seat National Assembly and the 90-seat National Council of Provinces with the NCOP consisting of 54 permanent members and 36 special delegates.
- Local government elected for 4 years; 284 metropolitan, district and local municipalities.
- Party List electoral system (200 from national party lists and 200 from party list in each of nine provinces).
- 13 political groups represented in National Assembly.
- The President is elected by the National Assembly. Under the SA Constitution, the President is permitted to serve a maximum of two five-year terms. Jacob Zuma elected President in May 2009. There is also a Deputy President.
- Constitution guarantees many rights including property rights and education; two-thirds of members of Parliament and at least 6 provinces need to support change to Constitution – ANC support in NA falls just short of this (65.9%).
- Success of ANC nationally and at provincial level since 1999 but support fell in 2009. Impact of Cope and gains for DA. Decline of IFP.
- In 2009 national election percentage of votes: ANC – 65.9%; DA – 16.6%; Cope – 7.4%.; IFP – 4.5%.
- ANC won majority in 8 of 9 provinces. DA won majority in W. Cape (22 of 44 seats).
- Seats in National Assembly 2009 were: ANC = 264 (-33 from 2004); DA = 67 (+20); Cope = 30 (new); IFP = 18 (–5). Altogether there are 13 parties represented in NA. 28 parties contested 2009 election.
- In 2006 local elections ANC polled the most votes in each of nine provinces (although lost position of power in Cape Town).
- After 2009 election DA had representation in all provinces.
- Effectiveness of opposition parties – arguably still somewhat fragmented and divided. Some evidence ANC tolerates opposition rather than respects.
- Concerns about ANC intolerance towards media opposition.
- Other relevant points.

Study Theme 3B – The People's Republic of China

Question C8

"Pass" and better answers should feature developed, exemplified knowledge and understanding of:

Sources of opposition to the Chinese Communist Party (CPC)
Extent of opposition within China as a whole
And
Balanced comment/analysis on the extent of opposition to the Communist Party in China.

Answers may refer to:
- Dissidents eg Hu Jia who was sent to prison for 3.5 years ahead of Olympic Games but few in number.
- Minorities eg Xinjiang and Tibet and related separatist movements. At least 140 people killed in rioting in Xinjiang (July '09).
- Provinces eg Guangdong has a reputation of not following central government directives.
- Hong Kong: 'One China Two Systems' and Taiwan's continued detachment from China. Former Hong Kong Governor Chris Patten sees China as threat to 'democracy' (11/08).
- Poor, unemployed/under-employed, landless. Up to 20m migrants forced to return to countryside as result of downturn in economy.
- Rise in levels of web-based dissent eg through blogs and chatrooms. High number of journalists under arrest but BBC website recently unblocked. Internationally China ranked very poorly in terms of internet/media freedom. Charter '08 document and on-line petition.
- Middle classes who have gained economic power and social status but no real political power.
- Crackdown on protest before and during Olympic Games.
- Numerous local and environmental protests involving crowds of up to 30,000. There were a total of 120,000 "mass incidents" in 2008. 2009 expected to be higher (20 years since Tiananmen Sq. protests/50 years of CPC rule).
- Greater criticism allowed of corrupt local officials. Renewed crackdown after Sichuan earthquake. Reaction to contaminated milk scandal.
- No general opposition to CPC; marginalised and disparate. Rises in the general standard of living have reduced criticism of CPC. Consensus is that there is little demand for political change.
- There are eight other political parties in China but are not in opposition to the CPC. Parties may participate in Government decisions but not allowed formal organisational status so can't raise funds or campaign.
- No free trade union association. ACFTU seen as tool of CPC.
- Treatment of members of Falun Gong.
- Wide range of powers available to Chinese authorities to silence political protestors. Arrest, imprisonment, house arrest, etc. Catch-all subversion, sedition and leaking of State secrets laws.
- Other relevant points.

Study Theme 3C – The United States of America

Question C9

"Pass" and better answers should feature developed, exemplified knowledge and understanding of:

The US immigration debate
The impact of immigration on US society (economic, social, political, cultural, regional)
And
Balanced comment/analysis on the impact overall of immigration on the USA.

Answers may refer to:
- US reputation as 'land of free' and history of immigration. Ethnic diversity is cause for celebration.
- Argument that immigrants stimulate the economy in terms of demand for housing, medical care, education and other services.
- Immigrants do many of the low paid jobs that Americans do not want; wages are suppressed and this keeps the US competitive. Many authorities in larger US cities have instructed enforcement personnel to not comply with federal agencies with regard to illegal immigrants in their jurisdiction.

- Most economists believe immigrants contribute more in the long-term than they cost to assimilate. Most immigrants are young, economically active and often skilled.
- Bush's 'Guest Worker' program attempted to recognise economic benefits of immigration by allowing US employers to sponsor non-US citizens, failed in Congress. Arizona (and other SW States) is considering setting up its own 'guest worker program'. Congress has tried and failed three times to pass an immigration bill.
- Argument that wages levels are forced down by immigrants. There is competition in employment, for housing, etc. Some economists argue that immigration benefits middle class most but hurts poor.
- Cost to US taxpayer for health care, education and welfare payments. 33% use at least one welfare program compared to 19% native.
- 'US culture' being overwhelmed. English no longer main language in many areas. Hispanics majority forecast in California by 2030. In 2008, there was an estimated 11-12m illegal immigrants in the US (30% rise since 2000 but numbers now falling). Many immigrants make no attempt to assimilate.
- In 2007, 37m people in the US were immigrants (1 in 8 of total population with 1 in 3 illegals). Over 1m people became US citizens in 2008.
- Huge investment in US border security; tighter restrictions on legal immigration. Obama plans to increase border security further. Various States have attempted to reduce access to welfare payments, etc. to illegal immigrants.
- Polls show most in US in favour of tighter controls. Hardening of attitudes especially post 9/11. Patriot Act (and renewal) makes it easier for US authorities to deny access to 'aliens'. Anti-immigration groups eg 'Minuteman'.
- Increase in size of minority ethnic vote and importance in 2008 US Presidential election. Nearly 70% of Hispanics voted for Obama.
- Other relevant points.

Study Theme 3D – The European Union

Question C10

"Pass" and better answers should feature developed, exemplified knowledge and understanding of:

The aims and structures of the CAP/CFP
Impact of both the CAP and CFP on EU member states
And
Balanced comment/analysis on the extent to which the CAP/CFP has benefited the member states of the European Union.

Answers may refer to:
- CAP – aims to secure food supplies, increase production and productivity, reduce dependency on imported food, stabilise prices, secure farms incomes and increase the overall standard of living of all those involved in agriculture.
- Seen as more favourable to some: France gets most out of CAP overall (20%); Ireland and Greece do best on per capita terms. Biggest farmers gain most. 80% of funds go to just 20% of farmers.
- Implications of enlargement especially cost. UK wants to end direct farm payments by 2015-2020 leaving the CAP aimed at protecting the environment.
- Has produced huge food surpluses over the years; cost of storage/destruction.
- 2009 cost EU €56bn; 43% of budget but falling proportionally since 1985; agricultural spending to be steady between 2006-13 despite increased EU membership; support given to farmers in older members States will be cut 8-9%.
- Only 5% of EU citizens work in agriculture (18% in Poland) producing 1.6% of EU's GDP; but proportion falling; halved in 15 older member states between 1980 and 2003.
- New member states get subsidies but only at 25% of rate of older member states.
- Price support subsidies falling as farmers increasingly given direct payments. Cereal farmers paid to take land out of cultivation. Rural development aid paid as an alternative to encourage rural farm diversification. Reforms in 2003/4 led to payments linked to food safety, animal welfare and environmental protection. Rural development funding to increase. Aim to cut export subsidies.
- CFP – adopted in 1983; reformed in 1992 and 2002 with the aim of preserving fish stocks and the fishing industry. Needed to combat overfishing, improve fishermen's incomes, preserve marine ecosystems and maintain supply of fish to European markets.
- Fishing less than 1% of EU's GDP; in 2007-13 states have €3.8bn to spend with member states deciding how their allocation will be spent; emphasis to be on fish stock recovery plans, inland fishing and aquaculture.
- Member states are each given a national quota (total allowable catches – TACs). This is decided by Council of Ministers.
- To limit the capture of small fish so that they can reproduce, technical rules have been adopted. Minimum mesh sizes have been fixed. Certain areas may be closed to protect fish stocks. Some fishing gears can be banned and more "selective" techniques, which facilitate the escape of young fish and limit the capture of other species, may be made compulsory. Minimum fish sizes are set, below which it is illegal to land fish. Catches and landings have to be recorded in special logbooks.
- Enforcement – the authorities in the Member States have to ensure that CFP rules are respected. There is also a Community Inspectorate. Their role is to ensure that all national enforcement authorities apply the same standards of quality and fairness in their enforcement however, enforcement criticised for not preventing landing of illegal catches ('blackfish'), and the abuse of use of quotas ('quota hopping').
- CFP unpopular with fishing communities which, it is argued, has not maintained fishing stocks. SNP wants an end to EU control over fisheries.
- Entrenched interests in Spain, France, Portugal and Greece have successfully resisted reform of CFP.
- In 2009, EU Commission reported that the EU had too many fishing boats and major cuts were needed to make fishing sustainable. In a Green Paper the Commission stated fishermen should also be given more responsibility for managing stocks as well as asking for ideas for a reformed CFP in 2013.
- Other relevant points.

Study Theme 3E – The Politics of Development in Africa

Question C11

"Pass" and better answers should feature developed, exemplified knowledge and understanding of:

The part played by the UN in promoting development in Africa
The factors that limit UN programmes in promoting development
And
Balanced comment/analysis on the extent to which the UN has been effective in promoting development.

Answers may refer to:
- The UNDP and Progress towards the Millennium Development Goals (MDG) of 2015.

- The UN agencies and their roles:
  - WHO: promotion of health is seen as crucial to development. Examples include eradication of polio with mass vaccination programme in Somalia, Kenya and Ethiopia. 3m children under 5 vaccinated.
  - UNESCO: promotion of education is also seen as crucial to successful long-term development.
  - ILO: aims to promote rights at work, encourage decent employment and enhance social protection.
  - UNFPA aims to reduce poverty and ensure that every person enjoys a life of health and opportunity.
  - UNIDO helps developing countries and economies in transition.
  - FAO and IFAD work to reduce hunger by giving direct support, sharing information and expertise, and undertaking research to improve food supplies.
  - World Food Programme (WFP).
- UNICEF – is not funded by UN but relies on donations. Works closely with UN agencies in responding to crises and promoting development.
- Co-operation between the IMF, the World Bank, the WTO and the UN to promote development.
- Partnerships with voluntary organisations.
- Extent of and access to fresh water supplies and impact on health. UN Development Report of 2006 states it will be 2040 before MDG for fresh water supply reached in sub-Saharan Africa.
- FAO reported a rise in the numbers (265m) of hungry in sub-Saharan Africa in 2009. Impact of rising food prices and lower employment levels.
- Extent of available health care. Long-term health problems created by malaria infection, HIV/AIDS, etc., affect the most economically active section of the population and slow development.
- MDG 2 (education provision) likely to be missed by 15 countries by 2015. Explanation of role of education in breaking the 'poverty cycle'.
- Climate change and impact on agriculture in marginal areas. Prediction that some staple foods eg maize production will decrease by 30% in future. Mismanagement of soil.
- Conflict. 20 major conflicts in Africa since 1960. In 2009, 13 countries affected eg Darfur. Huge obstacle to development – destruction and death, disruption to food supplies, financial cost, etc.
- Debt. G8 has cancelled debts of poorest 14 countries (estimated $200bn) but African countries still repay more in debt than receive in aid.
- Terms of world trade including price fluctuations affecting cash crops. Dumping of subsidised farm produce on local markets. Import tariffs and restrictions. Impact of 'Credit Crunch'.
- Corruption and land tenure issues eg Zimbabwe and collapse of economy. Legacy of colonisation.
- Political instability, military coups (DR of Congo) and economic mismanagement eg commentators have questioned the sustainability of Uganda's Poverty Eradication Action Plan.
- Divided views within UN membership towards best way forward; failure of many developed countries to give 0.7% of GNP to UN.
- Effect of natural disasters eg floods or drought.
- Other relevant points.

Study Theme 3F – Global Security

Question C12

"Pass" and better answers should feature developed, exemplified knowledge and understanding of:

The role of NATO
Extent to which NATO has been effective in achieving international peace and security

And

Balanced comment/analysis on the effectiveness of NATO in achieving international peace and security.

Answers may refer to:

- NATO has ensured W. Europe/Europe's security since 1949. Idea of 'collective defence' still relevant to existing, new and would-be members eg Ukraine. Membership has increased to 28 (Albania and Croatia 2009) and there are partnership agreements with many other countries eg Montenegro, which provide opportunities for defence co-operation.
- NATO provides forum for discussion of global issues which can reduce tension.
- Strategy of 'flexible response' adopted for 21st Century. Aims to deal with new crises both within and outwith North Atlantic area including ethnic violence, abuse of human rights, political instability, the spread of nuclear technology, terrorism and international crime.
- In 2002, NATO-Russia Council established to provide a framework for consultation on security issues.
- Peacemaking and peacekeeping roles (alongside EU or UN personnel) in Europe: Bosnia (IFOR/SFOR ended 2004); Kosovo (KFOR 1999 to present – 10,000 troops deployed 2009) and Macedonia (from 2001 to 2003).
- NATO had no direct role in Iraq but an international stabilisation force was deployed to help train Iraqi military personnel and develop the country's internal security institutions. Co-ordinated by US-led multinational force.
- Support to African Union in Darfur – Mission in Sudan (AMIS) 2005-2007.
- NATO no longer needed – an 'anachronism'.
- Undermines role of UN as primary world body for preventing/ending conflict.
- Dominated by US in terms of funding, troops and subsequent policy. Obama met Medvedev to discuss cuts in nuclear missile (July 09) arguably this is what matters not NATO.
- Continued widening of membership and disagreement over funding contributions (France & Germany) and troop deployment (eg Afghanistan) makes policy agreement more difficult.
- Afghanistan – Response to 9/11, 'war on terror'/Taliban/al-Qaeda. Aim to assist the Afghan authorities in providing security and stability. ISAF took over from US-led coalition in 2006. In 2008, there were 50,700 NATO troops from 41 countries. 2008 'worst year for violence for NATO'. 'Downward spiral' as Taliban has proved resilient. However, it is argued that Afghan economy has recovered and the country's infrastructure has improved. Obama's troop surge 2009 & 2010.
- NATO strength concerns Russia and it is argued that this has encouraged developments in arms technology (US missile defence system in Poland and Czech Republic); Russia "will think of retaliatory steps". Russia has resumed military flights off coast of Scotland and 'show of strength' in May Day parades (09). Russian fears of 'being surrounded' eg if Ukraine joins NATO.

- In 2008, Russian military involvement in Georgia (South Ossetia and Abkhazia) led to strongest condemnation from NATO but NATO has been unwilling to stop these territories from becoming 'independent' of Georgia.
- NATO ships active in Middle East (Gulf of Aden) to prevent piracy.
- Iran has tested Shahab missile system with range of 2000km (can reach Greece, etc.)
- Other relevant points.

MODERN STUDIES HIGHER
PAPER 2
2010

Question 1

Karen McDonald says, *"Year after year, male death rates are higher than female death rates for all causes and men have lower life expectancy across Scotland."*

Source C1(a) shows she is **incorrect** as far as male death rates are concerned as annually strokes kill more women.

But she is **correct** with regard to Source C1(b) as male life expectancy is lower than female life expectancy across Scotland.

Question 2

(a) Karen McDonald claims: *"Annually the number of males exceeding the recommended alcohol guidelines continues to increase."*

She is exaggerating because Source C2(a) shows the percentage of Scottish males exceeding recommended guidelines on alcohol intake is **falling**.

(b) William Walker claims that: *"In any event, more women now smoke than men in every age group."*

He is exaggerating as Source C2(b) shows that more men smoke in three of the six age groups eg 25-34 years age group male smokers 35% to female smokers 28%.

Question 3

William Walker says: *"Surveys show most men wanted Well Man Clinics open in the evenings and a majority were unhappy with the information they received."*

Source C3(b) shows William to be **correct** as most men (77%) would have liked to see Well Man Clinics open in the evening. Source C3(a) shows that he is **incorrect** as most men (85%) were happy with the information they received from Well Man Clinics.

Note: When answering questions 1 and 3 candidates must quote fully from the sources and provide evidence to support and oppose the view.

Question 4

Credit will be given for:

A style appropriate to a report (sub-headings, chapters, etc) with:
- an introduction that indicates an awareness of the role to be adopted and makes a clear recommendation
- developed arguments in support of the recommendation
- identification of and comment on (rebuttal of) counter arguments
- provision and use of appropriate background knowledge
- an overall conclusion.

Arguments for the proposal may feature:
- male health/death rates/life expectancy worse
- relatively small investment with long-term financial savings
- men not making full use of traditional GP services and need additional help to change lifestyles
- gender equality legislation means men should not be treated less favourably for services than women.

Argument against the proposal may feature:
- WMC don't reach the type of men who most need to change their lifestyles
- waste of scarce resources/not value for money
- priority should be policies to reduce poverty and economic inequality not men's health
- not all men agree correct approach to improving men's health.

Credit will also be given for background knowledge which may be developed from the following statements:

Source A
- Numerous reports prove that the health of men in this country is worse than the health of women.
- …recent equality legislation eg Gender Equality Duty, Equality Bill 2008/09, etc.
- …on those issues particular only to males.
- …the many educational health campaigns being run by the Scottish Government.
- …wider approach to health care that looks at tackling the various causes of Scotland's poor health.

Source B
- …Scotland's abysmal health record.
- … "nanny state" approach.
- …the Scottish Government needs to address the underlying causes of social and economic inequality.
- …the link between poverty and poor health has been well documented.
- …other health education programmes.

Other background knowledge may include:
- Details of Well Man Clinics pilot or in Eng. 'Health of Men Initiative'.
- Reports on social/economic health inequalities.
- Scottish health problems eg the Big 3 killers.
- Scottish Government policies to combat health inequalities eg phasing out prescription charges, P1-P3 free school meals, etc.
- Scottish Government health promotion campaigns on healthy living, curbing alcohol sales, the smoking ban, etc.
- Knowledge of communities with particular health issues eg East End of Glasgow and links with joblessness.
- Other relevant points.

MODERN STUDIES HIGHER PAPER 1 2011

Section A – Political Issues in the United Kingdom

Study Theme 1A – Devolved Decision Making in Scotland

Question A1

"Pass" and better answers should feature developed, exemplified knowledge and understanding of:

Opportunities for MSPs to take part in the decision making process.
Extent of the influence of MSPs on decision making in the Scottish Government.
And
Balanced comment/analysis of the extent to which MSPs influence decision making in the Scottish Government.

Answers may refer to:

- Principles of Scottish Parliament include openness, responsiveness and accountability.
- Scottish Parliament electoral system means that it is unlikely that one party will dominate. Most likely scenario is coalition or minority government. Influence of individual MSPs is arguably greater.
- SNP minority Government. Must rely on support of other parties to pass legislation. Defeated over trams, minimum alcohol pricing and plans to replace Council Tax with Local Income Tax. Had to drop plans for a Referendum Bill. Past difficulties in passing Finance Bills (Budgets): Conservative MSPs able to secure a commitment to extra police officers, etc.
- Agreement in 2007 between SNP and Scottish Green Party to co-operate although in 2009 Budget was passed with support from all parties except Greens.
- First Minister's Question Time (214 oral questions/9,744 written questions answered in Chamber 2009-10). Possible for opposition to influence decision making but FM has backing of Civil Service that puts opposition at disadvantage. Alex Salmond regarded as strong FM but can be held to account eg apology over so-called loss of 'tartan tax' powers.
- Questions to Ministers.
- Committees. There are around fifteen committees. Some are mandatory eg Equal Opportunities and Public Petitions. Others are subject committees eg Education and Long Life Learning. Range and scope of committees huge with inquires in recent years on the Scottish economy, tourism and child poverty in Scotland.
- Most MSPs are members of at least one committee. Committees conduct inquires and produce reports. Scrutinise Government legislation and have power to alter bills. Committees can put forward their own proposals for new legislation in the form of committee bills.
- The Commission on Scottish Devolution (Calman Commission) was set up by opposition parties to review devolution in Scotland. SNP Government did not support motion to set up.
- Scottish Government does not require legislation to implement all policy eg abolition of prescription charges or bridge tolls.
- Impact of S.P. elections. SNP majority Government 2011.

- MSPs have right to introduce legislation (Member's Bill). Patrick Harvie's Bill (Offences (Aggravation by Prejudice Act 2009)) was adopted by SG. However MacDonald's End of Life Assistance Bill, where MSPs had a free vote, was defeated.
- Other relevant points.

Study Theme 1B – Decision Making in Central Government

Question A2

"Pass" and better answers should feature developed, exemplified knowledge and understanding of:

Ways different groups outside Parliament seek to influence decision making in Central Government.
Extent of influence of different groups outside Parliament on decision making in Central Government.
And
Balanced comment/analysis on the view that some groups outside Parliament have more influence on decision making than others.
Answers may refer to:

- Use of the media campaigns, petitions, lobbying, rallies and demonstrations, publicity stunts eg those used by (New) Fathers 4 Justice campaign.
- Direct action eg fuel protests of 2000 and 2007; recent anti-capitalist protestors; student protestors.
- Backing of MPs by trade unions and private businesses.
- Use of internet including Facebook, Twitter and YouTube. MySociety on-line campaign played a part in ensuring MPs expenses would be released under FOI.
- Evidence to suggest numbers of PG and range of activities has risen in recent years.
- The influence of the media on decision making.
- Pressure groups extend opportunities for participation and provide channel of communication between government and people.
- Insider and outside groups. Insider groups have close links with government departments or other official bodies. They are trusted and negotiate quietly often out of sight so difficult to gauge their influence. Outsider groups which lack recognition seek to convert and mobilise public opinion using such tactics as demonstrations and rallies.
- Groups with larger memberships or more money, causes that are compatible with government views and or arise from specific circumstances (Snowdrop campaign) are more likely to be successful.
- Sectional/Interest exist to defend or promote interest of their members eg trade unions or National Farmers Union. Cause groups exist to promote a cause eg nuclear disarmament or the abolition of blood sports.
- Success of high profile Ghurka campaign led by Joanna Lumley and of trade unions campaign to prevent part-privatisation of Royal Mail. Success of others, such as Jamie Oliver's campaign to improve quality of food to school pupils, are more difficult to determine.
- Cash-for-influence affair (similar to MPs Cash for Questions affair in the 1990s).
- 1.7m people signed e-petition on Downing Street website in 2007. In 2009, government decided to scrap plans for a national road charge scheme.
- Failure to Save the Scottish Regiments campaign.
- Arguably, internet-based pressure convinced the UK Government to open up MPs expenses to public scrutiny.
- Influence of senior civil servants.
- References to influences on peers in the House of Lords.
- Other relevant points.

Study Theme 1C – Political Parties and their Policies (including the Scottish Dimension)

Question A3

"Pass" and better answers should feature developed, exemplified knowledge and understanding of:

The ways in which party leaders are elected.
The importance of the party leader in achieving electoral success.
And
Balanced comment/analysis on the view that the choice of party leader is crucial to electoral success.

With reference to at least two political parties, **answers may refer to:**

Conservatives
- Two stage election process since 1998: system established by William Hague. Stage 1 involves Conservative MPs voting in secret until two candidates left. Stage 2 involves party members in postal vote between two candidates (OMOV).
- Election is triggered by resignation of Party Leader or by 15% of Conservative MPs writing to Chairman of the 1922 Committee supporting a motion of no confidence in the leader.
- If leader gets simple majority of Parliamentary Party (51%+) then no election challenge can be made for twelve months. If leader loses vote of no confidence, leader resigns and cannot stand in the election which follows. David Cameron elected leader December 2005.
- Nominated for leadership passed to Chairman of 1922 Committee.
- Procedures for electing Scottish Conservative leader.

Labour
- When in opposition, leadership election is triggered by 12.5% of the parliamentary Labour Party.
- When in government, election requires two thirds support of party conference votes.
- Since 1993, leader chosen by electoral college comprising of three equal sections: Labour MPs and members of the EU parliament, constituency party members and trade unions affiliated to the Party.
- Election based on principle of One Member One Vote (OMOV).
- Within constituency section, every CLP has one vote which is given to the leadership candidate who wins ballot of individual members.
- Within the trade union section, every affiliated trade union is given a share of the overall trade union vote based on size of trade union membership. Every affiliated trade union hold a postal ballot of its members and its electoral college votes are divided between the candidates according to their share of the postal ballot.
- Procedures for electing Scottish Labour leader.

Liberal Democrats
- Any MP can stand provided they have backing of at least 7 colleagues and 200 party members from 20 different constituencies. Election by STV. All 73,000 party members entitled to vote.
- Nick Clegg narrowly elected leader October 2007.
- Procedures for electing Scottish Liberal Democrat leader.

Scottish National Party
- Leader and deputy leader elected by simple majority. Alex Salmond polled 75% of vote in September 2004 election (Nicola Sturgeon 54% of vote for deputy).

- Analysis of importance of party leader in achieving electoral success:
  - Cameron is widely held to have improved Conservative fortunes. He has tried to embody the deeper changes the Conservatives have made to their policies and image; more inclusive and less 'nasty'.
  - Apart from a brief 'Brown bounce' in September 2008 at the start of the economic crisis, Brown's leadership is widely seen to be a liability to Labour's electoral success. There have been frequent rumbling of a leadership challenge culminating in the 'coup that never was' in June 2009.
  - Salmond is widely seen as an asset to the SNP. A shrewd politician who dominates the Scottish Parliament. The SNPs electoral fortune picked up after returned to the membership in 2004. In contrast, neither Iain Gray nor Tavish Scott have had much of an impact. Annabel Goldie has been a better performer on TV and in the Scottish Parliament but not enough to revive fortunes of Scottish Conservatives.
- Other relevant points.

Study Theme 1D – Electoral Systems, Voting and Political Attitudes

Question A4

"Pass" and better answers should feature developed, exemplified knowledge and understanding of:

The factors affecting voting behaviour.
The relative importance of different factors affecting voting behaviour.
And
Balance comment/analysis on the view that some of the factors affecting voting behaviour are more important than others.

Answers may refer to:
- A range of factors are said to affect voting behaviour including:
  - Media.
  - Social class.
  - Age.
  - Gender.
  - Residence.
  - Ethnicity.
  - Image of party leader.
  - Issues.
- Candidates who integrate factors will be credited highly. For example, social class and media can be seen as separate factors but they are related. Professional class voters may cross different newspapers, television and websites from lower class voters and are therefore exposed to a different set of media influences.
- Models of voting behaviour including social structures model and rational choice model. Debate as to extent to which rational choice model has taken social structures model. Some commentators (Sarlvik and Crewe) argue that absolute class voting and relative class voting have steadily declined and that 'issue voting' has become more important. Others (Heath) argue that although class voting has declined it remains the most important underlying factor affecting voting behaviour. The most recent studies (Manza, Hunt and Brooks) agree more with Heath.
- Tactical voting.
- Dealignment.
- Third party choices.
- Non-voting.

- Evidence of voting patterns from 2010 UK General Election (or other elections).
- Discussion of relative importance of different factors eg importance of Iraq War in relation to Muslim vote 2005, emphasis placed on successful media campaign by political parties, impact of 'economic crisis/recession', etc.
- Other relevant points.

Section B – Social Issues in the United Kingdom

Study Theme 2 – Wealth and Health Inequalities

Question B5

"Pass" and better answers should feature developed, exemplified knowledge and understanding of:

The link between poverty and health.
Other factors that may also affect health.
And
Balanced comment/analysis on the view that poverty is the most important factor that affects good health.

Answers may refer to:
- Health reports including 'Equally Well' (2008); annual 'Health in Scotland' reports; research from Glasgow Centre for Population Health; WHO Lenzie/Calton Report 2008, etc.
- Statistics in terms of mortality and morbidity. Scottish Government figures show that in 2007:
  - average life expectancy for males in Scotland was 74.9 but only 57.3 years in most deprived area. East Dunbartonshire was 78.0 years for males
  - under 75 deaths from heart disease and cancer were markedly higher in most deprived areas.
- Impact of low income:
  - welfare dependency
  - poor housing
  - run down local environment and effect on physical and mental health
  - Oxfam's 'FRED': Forgotten, Ripped off, Excluded, Debt.
- Harry Burns' research on 'biology of poverty'. Experience of being brought up in 'chaotic circumstances' has an effect on the body's immune system leading to a more unhealthy life, longer recovery from illnesses/operations and lower life expectancy.
- Other factors may include:
  - lifestyle choices (inc. smoking, alcohol, diet, drug misuse and exercise)
  - hereditary factors
  - gender
  - race
  - availability and uptake of preventative medical care
  - access to private medical acre.
- Candidates who avoid over simplification and acknowledge that certain health issues transcend class differences eg alcohol misuse or lack of exercise will be credited highly.
- Other relevant points.

Question B6

"Pass" and better answers should feature developed, exemplified knowledge and understanding of:

Government health and welfare provision.
The debate over government/individual responsibility for health and welfare.
And
Balanced comment on/analysis as to whether or not health and welfare provision should be the responsibility of government.

Answers may refer to:
- UK and Scottish Government health and welfare provision may include:
  - National Health Service
  - Benefits – JSA, State Retirement Pension, Pension Credit, Child Benefit, Income Support, Employment Support Allowance, tax credits, free prescriptions in Scotland, etc.
- Founding principles of the Welfare State – universalism with flat-rate contributions (NI) giving 'cradle to grave' coverage.
- Debate over extent of government health and welfare provision. Individualism and collectivism. Individualists stress importance of self-reliance and need to avoid a 'dependency culture' whereas collectivists stress importance of fairness and equality in society.
- Labour's 'Third Way' – policy of 'welfare to work'. Welfare Reform Bill 2009 aims to further support people back into work as putting more responsibility on claimants to move towards work or lose benefit.
- Increased use of means testing welfare system against a background of rising costs.
- Impact of an ageing population. Future rises in ratio of dependents to workers.
- Widening of health and wealth gaps between most and least affluent.
- Strong public support for NHS. 2009 opinion poll in Guardian suggests public want NHS to be protected from future public expenditure cuts.
- SNP Scottish Government has been collectivist in approach eg free prescriptions and free school meals P1-3.
- Major political parties agree that health and welfare provisions is the responsibility of both the Government and the individual. The role of Government is to help the individual help themselves.
- 2009, Labour has proposed extending 'free' social care for the elderly in their own homes in England and Wales.
- Cameron's view on welfare – big government is wasteful and fails; talks of 'social entrepreneurs and community action'; proposed reforms to NHS in England and Wales; challenges to idea of 'Big Society'.
- Other relevant points.

Section C – International Issues

Study Theme 3A – The Republic of South Africa

Question C7

"Pass" and better answers should feature developed, exemplified knowledge and understanding of:

Government policies to reduce social and economic inequalities. Extent to which government policies have been effective in reducing social and economic inequalities.

And

Balanced comment/analysis of the effectiveness of government policies to reduce social and economic inequalities.

Answers may refer to:
- Black Economic Empowerment (BEE) is main growth strategy. Introduced in 2003 it also aims to ensure all South Africans have equality of opportunity. Operates through series of codes of practice (adopted 2007). Replaced GEAR (1996-2000) which aimed to develop SA economy through promotion of more open market, privatisation and increased foreign investment. This policy had only limited success.
- Accelerated and Shared Growth initiative aims to halve poverty and unemployment by 2014.
- Expanded Public Works Programme to create one million work opportunities by 2009.
- National Skills Fund widened to assist young, unemployed and lesser skilled.
- Increased in spending on education and health. Number of students in Higher education to 750,000. Most South Africans now live within 5km of health facility.
- Programmes to ensure everyone has access to drinkable water, sanitation and electricity.
- Inequalities within and between races in terms of housing, health, income, poverty, education, employment/unemployment, crime and health.
- Gini co-efficient for South Africa has widened in recent years (0.6) with inequalities growing fastest amongst blacks (0.64).
- In 2007, 80% of people had electricity in home (58% 1996), 70% water in home (61%), 71% sanitation (50%).
- SA Government figures show 40% of people live in poverty – more than half surviving on less than one dollar a day. UN figure is higher with most being black.
- White unemployment is around 8% but Black unemployment may be as high as 50%.
- Increase in black middle class ('Black Diamonds') to 2.6m. Black representation reached 22% in top management in 2007.
- Decrease in income poverty for most South Africans but increase in levels of white South African poverty.
- Average white household salary 5.5 times the average black salary (2008) but difference falling.
- 2.3m new houses completed with 3.1m housing subsidises provided to improve housing.
- Government target of delivering 30% of agricultural land to black majority unlikely to be met as only 5% redistributed by 2007.
- SA described as "45/55" society – 45% in poverty and 55% not.
- Inequalities between provinces – Guateng wealthiest province, Eastern Cape poorest.
- Economic impact of 2010 World Cup.
- Other relevant points.

Study Theme 3B – The People's Republic of China

Question C8

"Pass" and better answers should feature developed, exemplified knowledge and understanding of:

Social and economic change.
Impact of social and economic change.

And

Balanced comment/analysis of the extent to which social and economic change has benefited the people of China.

Answers may refer to:
- Market economy has been steadily developing since early 1980s. Encouragement of individual initiatives and entrepreneurship.
- China joined World Trade Organisation in 2001. Third largest economy in world (US $4.32 trillion 2008).
- Introduction of Household Responsibility System. Today most farms operate as private businesses.
- Dismantling of work permit system (hukou).
- Foreign investment, encouragement of private business, changes to banking system.
- In 2009, Hu stated that China will continue to develop its 'socialist market economy' although US did not recognise China as a market economy at that time.
- Recession has seen government establish control over some privately owned businesses eg in airlines, steel and coal industry.

- Majority in China has benefited from social and economic reform but all have not benefited equally.
- Rise in average per capita income to $4644 (2009).
- Richest 10% of Chinese population account for 33.1% of consumption, poorest 10% only 1.8%.
- In 2009, 43m Chinese people below revised poverty line of 1,100 yuan per year but big decrease from 200m in poverty in 1978.
- A World Bank report 2006 stated income of bottom 10% of Chinese people had decreased by 2.4% in that year.
- Urban rural contrasts. Between 2005-07, one-third of rural households experienced poverty. Urban incomes growing at between 10-15% per year, far higher than rural incomes.
- Availability of private health care and private education.
- Environmental pollution and loss of land, housing, etc for some groups of people.
- Increase in corruption, crime, and other social ills of capitalist society.
- Hu's promotion of 'Harmonious Society' partly reflects CPC's concerns with growing inequality.
- Development of social security system.
- Increase in use of mobile phones and internet users. There is greater access to information on-line but many websites remain blocked eg Twitter.
- Constitution guarantees private property.
- 20m migrants have lost jobs as a result of the global economic crisis.
- Changes in some areas to one-child policy.
- Constitution guarantees religious freedom but little religious freedom in practice.
- Highest income groups in urban areas earn 5.6 times salary of lowest income groups.
- Other relevant points.

Study Theme 3C – The United States of America

Question C9

"Pass" and better answers should feature developed, exemplified knowledge and understanding of:

Government policies to reduce social and economic inequalities. Extent to which government policies have been effective in reducing social and economic inequalities.
And
Balanced comment/analysis of the effectiveness of government policies to reduce social and economic inequalities.

Answers may refer to:

- US Government/State welfare programmes. Most mainly funded by federal government but usually administered by state government includes:
  - Medicare, Medicaid and State Children's Health Insurance Program (covers children who do not qualify for Medicaid)
  - Temporary Assistance for Needy Families (TANF) introduced as part of Welfare Reform Act 1996 and ties welfare payments to the search for work. Limited to five years for cash support
  - Food stamps
  - Affirmative Action programmes as they apply today
- American Recovery and Reinvestment Act 2009 – economic stimulus package worth $787bn. $82bn of package is to provide for expansion of unemployment benefits, social welfare provision, education and health care.
- Some States have more generous programmes of welfare support than others.
- No Child Left Behind (NCLB) 2001 – aimed to improve performance in public schools to improve qualifications/employability of all children. Backed with big increases in federal funding but on-going debate as to success.
- US has a rising Gini coefficient rating of over 0.4 one of the highest amongst developed nations.
- In 2007, Congressional Budget Office study found that incomes rose by 35% in some families affected by 1996 changes in US Government welfare to work programmes. On the other hand, many other families, many of which are black have experienced increased poverty.
- Race, gender and geographic inequalities in terms of housing, income, poverty rates, health, crime, education and employment/unemployment, etc.
- Success of minority groups and others – creation of Black middle class, Hispanic and Asian businesspeople, some Asian groups in terms of education, etc., do better than Whites.
- The debate over Affirmative Action.
- Prevailing individualist view within US society and that it is not government's responsibility to reduce social and economic inequality.
- Impact of Obama's proposed healthcare reforms which, if successful, would reduce the social inequality of access to healthcare.
- Other relevant points.

Study Theme 3D – The European Union

Question C10

"Pass" and better answers should feature developed, exemplified knowledge and understanding of:

The main social and economic policies of the EU and their agreed aims.
Social and economic policy on which there is disagreement within the EU.
And
Balanced comment/analysis of the extent of disagreement on social and economic policy among member states on the EU.

Answers may refer to:

- Enlargement – Seven potential new members to existing 27. Croatia likely to join 2011. Others, including Turkey which started negotiations for entry in 2005, will take longer. The Ukraine and Georgia have also been talked about as future members of the EU.
- Common Agricultural and Fisheries Policy. Disagreement over cost, implementation, success, etc.
- Monetary union – In 2009, 22 countries were using the euro with more to follow. Only the UK, Denmark and Sweden have not moved to the euro.
- EU Budget – 133.8bn euros in 2009. Most spent on agricultural subsidies and rural development (47% of total spend) and regional aid (32%).
- Working Time Directive and the opt-out. UK is continuing to resist pressure to end its opt-out from the maximum 48-hour working week.
- Lisbon Treaty/Reform Treaty – mainly political reform of EU but as new treaty amends Treaty on the European Union (Maastricht) and Treaty of Rome (established EC) credit. Includes new powers to EC, EP and European Court of Justice with regard to justice and home affairs.
- Disagreement between different political blocs (liberals, socialists, etc.) as well as between stages eg over immigration/free movement of labour.

- Enlargement debate. Supporters of further EU enlargement highlight the economic benefits of bigger EU market. The EU is now the single biggest market in the world. Opponents have concerns over impact of further enlargement in respect of cost and decision making.
- Disputes between member nations over CAP and CFP. Some countries such as France, Ireland and Greece do well from CAP. New EU members getting less from CAP than older EU members. Supporters of CAP say it is vital to rural communities, others argue costs too much and benefits relatively few people. EU Commission aims to bring a reformed CFP into existence by 2013.
- UK (and other) rebate.
- 2008 accord struck on the detention and deportation of illegal immigrants after years of disagreement.
- Lisbon Treaty/Reform Treaty came into force 2009. Aims to streamline EU institutions to make EU operate more efficiently. Ireland, Denmark and the UK will have right to opt in our out of any new policies in the area of justice and home affairs. Poland may also eventually opt out from charter of Fundamental Rights.
- Other relevant points.

Study Theme 3E – The Politics of Development in Africa

Question C11

"Pass" and better answers should feature developed, exemplified knowledge and understanding of:

The importance of education and health care on development. Other factors that influence development.
And
Balanced comment/analysis of the importance of health and education overall in securing successful development in Africa.

*For this question, candidates must demonstrate specific knowledge of at **least one** African country.*

Answers may refer to:
- Extent of education/health provision in developing countries in Africa. May be taken from a variety of sources eg UN Development reports. Reference can be made to:
  - low levels of adult literacy
  - low level of school enrolment
  - high levels of illiteracy
  - low level of expenditure on health and education (public and private) in both actual and percentages terms
  - low life expectancy
  - infant/child mortality rates
  - other related measures of health and education development.

- Education and health are seen as fundamental to a country's economic and social development.
- Examples of improved education/health care and link to increase levels of development.
- The Millennium Development Goals (MDGs).

- Other relevant factors that influence development include:
  - good governance
  - terms of trade
  - conflict
  - debate
  - aid and international investment
  - types of levels of natural resources.

- Other relevant points.

Study Theme 3F – Global Security

Question C12

"Pass" and better answers should feature developed, exemplified knowledge and understanding of:

The ways the UN deals with threats to international peace and security.
The debate over reform on the UN.
And
Balanced comment/analysis of the view that the UN must reform to be more effective when dealing with threats to international peace and security.

Answers may refer to:
- In 2008, UN Secretary-General Ban Ki-moon outlined plans for reform of the UN. He sought to strengthen UN's capacity for preventative diplomacy as well as increase UN's ability to support peace efforts once conflict had ceased.
- There are fifteen of UN's Security Council, five of which are permanent – the P5 who have power of veto – with the other ten members elected.
- General Assembly Task Force on Security Council Reform encompasses a variety of proposals, such as eliminating the veto held by the five permanent members, and expansion of the Council.
- On-going discussions with regard to financial contributions/spending.
- Calls for the UN to have a force of its own.

- View that it is easier to be critical of the UN rather than see where it has been 'quietly successful' eg Cyprus, Kashmir, Liberia and the Democratic Republic of Congo. In 2009, the UN had 17 on-going peace missions around the world.
- Criticism of UN in respect of Bosnia, Rwanda, Somalia, Kosovo and Darfur.
- View that although UN's institutional arrangements are complex, the real problem for the UN is that its members are deeply divided about what they want from it.
- UN largely ignored by USA (and other countries) in respect of Iraq.
- North Korea and Iran's continued defiance of UN with regard to nuclear capability.
- Style of UN Security-General. Kofi Annan very high profile and wishing to be seen to be involved. Ban Ki-moon more low-key working hard in the background.
- Responses to terrorism – UN Global Counter = Terrorism Strategy.
- In 2001, UN Security Council authorised US to overthrow the Taliban in Afghanistan and for US and allies to set up the International Security Assistance Force (ISAF).

- Other relevant points.

MODERN STUDIES HIGHER
PAPER 2
2011

Question 1

Ken Dorward states, *"However, since 2007, the number of people on low incomes has risen while the relative value of the NMW in the UK is one of the lowest in the developed world."*

Source C1 shows he is **correct** as the number of people on low incomes has started to rise from 2007.

But he is **incorrect** with regard to Source C2 as the relative value of the NMW in the UK is not one of the lowest in the developed world. The UK lies fourth behind France, Australia and the Netherlands.

Question 2

Ken Dorward states, *"Few people believe that an £8 per hour NMW will push up wage rates in other areas of employment."*

Ken exaggerates because Source C3 shows 40% of people surveyed believe a higher NMW will push up wages in other areas of employment. This is highest percentage response.

Question 3

Christine Kelly states that, *"The UK now has very few households living in poverty compared to other European Union countries."*

Christine exaggerates because Source C4 shows UK is fourth highest in table just below Greece, Italy and Spain. UK is also above EU average.

Question 4

Christine Kelly states, *"Opinion surveys show that the public agree with the idea of a NMW but an £8 NMW but an £8 NMW would have a disastrous affect on a businesses such as hotels and restaurants where the majority of low paid workers are found."*

Source C3 shows Christine to be correct as 85% of people surveyed agreed with the idea of a NMW.

Source C5 shows that she is incorrect as only 12% of low paid workers are found in hotels and restaurants.

Note: When answering questions 1 and 4 candidates must quote fully from the sources and provide evidence to support and oppose the view.

Question 5

Decision Making Task or Report
- The report **must** feature background knowledge to pass
- Use must be made of all specified sources

A style appropriate to a report (sub-headings, chapters etc) with:
- an introduction that indicates an awareness of the role to be adopted and makes a clear recommendation
- developed arguments in support of the recommendation
- identification of and comment on (rebuttal of) counter arguments
- provision and use of appropriate background knowledge
- an overall conclusion.

Arguments for the proposal may feature:
- poverty levels rising; help meet poverty targets and end poverty wages
- reduce social inequalities – collectivist approach
- simplified tax and benefit system
- stimulate economy
- make work 'pay' and encourage workforce to become more skilled

Argument against the proposal may feature:
- harm economic recovery; hurt business relative to foreign competition
- unjustified: UK NMW relatively high
- individualist approach best way to tackle poverty and reduce inequality
- employees should be paid only what they are worth
- increase wages across employment levels

Credit will also be given for background knowledge which may be developed from the following statements:

Source A
- "…government…targets to reduce poverty…"
- "…a collectivist approach…"
- "…the social problems poverty creates…"
- "…extent to which society has become more divided has become all too clear."
- "complicated and costly process of means-tested benefits could be scrapped…"
- "Many politicians believe the NMW is too low."

Source B
- "…worst recession in fifty years…"
- "The rates of pay for the NMW currently ensure there are no poverty wages in this country."
- "…range of benefits and government programmes to support the poorest groups in society."
- "…dependency culture…"
- "multinational companies…"
- "…UK unemployment rates are historically high…"

Other background knowledge may include:
- Number and types of workers currently benefiting from NMW
- Year NMW introduced/details of NMW 16-17 or 18-20
- The individualist/collectivist debate
- Consequences of widening social and economic inequalities
- Extension of adult NMW to 21 year olds 2010

Hey! I've done it

BrightRED
PUBLISHING

© 2011 SQA/Bright Red Publishing Ltd, All Rights Reserved
Published by Bright Red Publishing Ltd, 6 Stafford Street, Edinburgh, EH3 7AU
Tel: 0131 220 5804, Fax: 0131 220 6710, enquiries: sales@brightredpublishing.co.uk,
www.brightredpublishing.co.uk

Official SQA answers to 978-1-84948-209-7
2007-2011